THE BOOK OF
LOVE & LOSS
POEMS FOR TODAY

With grateful thanks
for their generosity to Parkinson's
research and this anthology to:
Octagon Consultancy
Professional Financial Advice
Clifton, Bristol

and Acumen Literary Journal
edited by Patricia Oxley MBE
whose kind contribution
has facilitated the launch of the anthology
at The 2014 Torbay Poetry Festival

Also a warm thank you to the many authors
represented in this anthology who have extensively
supported it not only by offering their excellent poetry
to a worthwhile charitable enterprise but also
by subsequently acting as lively
ambassadors for the book

Thanks too to the various professionals
whose enthusiasm, skills and advice
have helped the editors in the areas of design
and production, printing, promotion, sales,
distribution, publicity and sponsorship

THE BOOK OF

LOVE & LOSS

POEMS FOR TODAY

Edited by
RV Bailey & June Hall

BELGRAVE
PRESS·BATH

First Edition: The Book of Love and Loss
First published in Great Britain in 2014 by
The Belgrave Press, Bath,
7 Belgrave Rd, Bath, BA1 6LU.

(No unsolicited submissions please)

R V Bailey and June Hall have asserted their right under the
Copyright, Designs and Patents Act 1988 to be identified as the
authors of this selection of work.

ISBN 978-0-9546215-2-0

British Library Cataloguing in Publication Data.
A CIP record for this book can be obtained from the British Library.

Designed and typeset by John Hawkins Design 01424 423859
Cover designed by Paul Mitchell Design Ltd 01628 664011

Printed in Zrinski d.d., Croatia

Dedicated to the memory of

U A Fanthorpe

1929 – 2009

CONTENTS

7

8

16

❧ FOREWORD ❧

A book of poems on love and loss? Yes, I'll write an introduction, I told the unknown voice on the phone. *Send me some examples of the poems, would you?* I thought I'd check them first, for readability.

The bundle of A4 arrived post hasty, and lay on my desk, through a week of sit-com angst and interviews on Hull until today, when I picked them up and accompanied by a mug of green tea skimmed through them.

The first poem I read was by Simmons – *for Hugh*, and the first line read:

> *I am keeping this room swept until you come back.*

And suddenly I was gulping tea through a swollen throat, and tears were billowing – billowing down my face, lodging in my specs, dropping from my chin.

May 29th was the day; 2004 was the year. I've had ten whole years to get over my Love and Loss. Surely, 'billowing' was a bit over the top, wasn't it?

I swam to the next verse. Wanda Barford wrote:

> *I'd love to phone you*
> *And tell you what's been happening…*
>
> *…Goodness knows what the cost would be*
> *over such a long distance.*

And I began to whimper pathetically, like a dog left in a car, and to howl, the way you only can when you're alone. And I've had ten whole years this May to pull myself together.

When Jack died, I stopped reading fiction. My imagination died with him. I was always such a reader – *Voracious* was my adjective. *She's always got her nose in a book*, my Mother repeated, as though it was an affliction she had to bear. And Enid Blyton, Lorna Hill, Austen and Eliot provided all my role models.

Only now I had my nose in a box of tissues, and real life was stranger than any fiction.

It took two years for help to arrive in the form of poetry, for Penelope Shuttle and Dannie Abse to do the search-and-rescue on me, in such particular words and precise thoughts to show me I was not alone. And gently, with tough love, they and other poets more or less saved my life.

These pages of poetry are a pace-maker for the broken heart.

Maureen Lipman
2014

❧ INTRODUCTION ❧

Perhaps life draws its dynamic from the constant re-balancing of Love and Loss. Loss stalks all our days, some of it secret, some private, some shared... [It] alters the very shape of one's psyche, leaving one always diminished. (Pam Leighton)

Love and loss must surely be the most significant experiences in most people's lives. Neither can be predicted, and neither, perhaps, avoided. The first is altogether life-enhancing: to be able to love someone, and to be loved by that someone – these things set the world on fire. You are blessed beyond words. Simply because you are human, you may know love, and poets have celebrated this state of affairs with enthusiasm since writing began. You will find some of the happiest contemporary love poems here.

But once you know love, you are doomed. For you are a hostage to fortune: the greater the love, the greater the grief of loss, and just as suddenly, the world can change again. To lose that pearl of great price, having once so miraculously found it, is a mortal blow. At first, shocked by the finality of the event itself, you don't realise the full implications of what has happened. Then it comes home to you: happiness, as you knew it – have known it, perhaps, for a lifetime – has gone for ever. The past-ness of the past is unbearably painful. Housman put it well:

That is the land of lost content,
I see it shining plain,
The happy highways where I went
And cannot come again.

People back off from you, as if grief were infectious. Friends mean well, but confronted by the enormity of such misery, they are rendered inarticulate: they simply *don't know* what to say. The kindest ones don't use words at all, they just hug you.

What words do come are often platitudes, which don't help. Platitudes have been around for a long time: Hamlet's mother, Gertrude (being Shakespearian), must be the most distinguished of the devotees of the platitude. Here she is, telling off Hamlet for minding so much about his father's death, and for (as she sees it) making a fuss.

Thou know'st 'tis common: all that live must die
Passing through nature to eternity.

When Hamlet responds: *Ay madam, it is common,* Gertrude pushes the point home matter-of-factly:

If it be, why seems it so particular with thee?

But of course it *is* particular, it is special to each one of us. *No one has ever suffered so terribly...we never knew it was possible to hurt so much and still be alive...*

In such moments of deep unhappiness most of us turn to books for a sense of companionship. We try to find other people's words, other people's experiences, that may legitimise and perhaps distance what we feel. Perhaps these writers felt what we feel; perhaps they may be able to help us make sense of this chill world, where we are suddenly lost, suddenly strangers.

When Princess Diana died, hundreds of ordinary people put their grief into words. And what they wrote was not prose. They may not have written very well, but they knew instinctively that what was needed was poetry – poems seem the natural currency for grief. And poets, more than other writers, seem to know what to say.

Bereaved people need to talk to a friend who understands what they are feeling, and it's not easy to find someone who can say to you the words you need to hear, when grief sweeps your life away. Poets however do seem to know what to say. There is a strong elegiac line in English poetry, and poems from the past may console, if you can find them. But contemporary poets may have more to offer, in that they speak the same language as we do; they speak more directly to us, they live in the world where we live. Theirs is the heightened diction of poetry, but it is also recognisably our diction.

Pat Borthwick wrote: *I know how important talking to one another is, and I hope that this selection of poems talks to the readers, and shows them that we are all a community of those who grieve.*

Not only Pat: all these poets talk to us, in their different voices – the tight-lipped, and the wordy: those who ramble in the desperate homeless way that grief induces. Those whose love rushes at the reader through a torrent of everyday detail, and those whose grief is dumbstruck; those who can cope only with the memory of the past, and those who have caught the rope, perhaps by a single word, that will haul them into their future – *...something / that justifies our coming and going.*

One poem celebrates a 'good' death; but there's also the death that's happened though no one yet knows about it. All deaths are the same – yet all deaths are different: the smashed bicycle, the car accident, the Twin Towers; the death in wartime at sea; the death that occurred in another time zone, when the parents were asleep. Deaths at home, in hospital, of parents and partners and children; the passing of damaged babies, and babies born dead; the death of animals – horses, dogs, cats – and, of course, the part played by animals in comforting. Losing one's home is a kind of death; so is the break-up of a close relationship. It is hard to come to terms with the loss of health, or the loss of your job, and all that it meant to you.

Suddenly you're in a play you've never learnt the lines for, whose cast are strangers; and each act in the drama is a different kind of nightmare, from the initial shock of hearing the news, perhaps by a voice on the phone, to coming to terms, after the fuss and the funeral, with a changed life. These poets know about it, at every stage, and their words are the authentic signals of suffering. Their insights lie behind what follows in this collection.

They know how it is to miss someone close: how *no one now can understand your special language*; how no one recognises that now, in fact, you're blind, deaf, drowning in grief – though there's no white stick, no hearing-aid to show, and your only physical symptom is a stone in your throat that can't be swallowed.

They know that who you're missing isn't just anyone, but someone unique: your 'wit-reflector' with the 'beloved grin'. Suddenly you discover that you are *one*, no longer half of a couple, you are *a different person and a different pronoun. And how you disappear*, says one writer: ' *I have become used to not being seen'*.

There are mysteries. How your hands miss their counterparts – the *hand still reaching out to touch your hand, knowing it is not there.* Time and reality are distorted: *how can the world still go on, the sky be blue?*

You learn how seductive grief is, how mad, in the rage it can call forth, the self-reproach. Not all comforters are like Lady Macbeth, but you do learn how awkward is grief, for both sufferer and comforter. What you actually hope for ('no exhortations', no advice about 'letting go') is just 'the occasional touch of a hand'. Perhaps the Russians got it right; a special room for weeping provided at Chernobyl, where it was OK to howl.

But you haven't time to howl: there is so much to do, not least the turning of feeling into fact, as you register the death. Perhaps you must endure the funeral unseen, an unacknowledged lover *small with grief*, who has no proper place, who stands alone.

Then coming back to the empty slippers, the silent telephone, the hairpins, the watch and the walking-stick; how to dispose of what's left – their ashes; their clothes, their precious things. The house clearance in the rain. The shredder. We inherit 'not the chiffonier' but houses-without-their-owners; the loneliness of the solitary inmate; the empty kitchen and the stopped clock; the hollow ring and the empty bed.

But there are also elements of comedy, of affectionate absurdities – perhaps in the end what touch us most aren't 'careful words' but the ordinary things we find, like rubber bands, green balls of string. Loved ones can remain strangely alive – on Google, and in so many other ways, in the eloquence of their clothes or belongings, their familiar words and phrases, in the powerful reality of dreams. You may treasure the clothes they gave you, wear them again, covering yourself in their love.

For love has transforming power. Grief is like an animal, determined, persuasive, irresistible; but in the end it is love that wins, for love, unlike grief, goes on. The bereaved are braver than they know, refusing to grieve but also refusing to be persuaded not to grieve. They know they need strategies to manage grief: *If I get to six o'clock I'll pour myself a drink …Tonight I'm doing well… This is going to be one of those days when I don't cry…* They learn to recognise the signs of spring, the signals that begin to lift the heart, the moment when it's possible to rearrange the furniture. Ultimately humanity keeps faith with the past, refuses loss, time and again rebuilding cathedrals, cities destroyed by war; and in the cemeteries you will come across the lonely men *whose busyness hints almost at cheerfulness.* At the start it is impossible. But there is wit, and courage; there's the attempt to imagine what heaven's like.

There are poems here about all sorts of bereavement and poems that try to make sense of unbearable loss; poems that can speak the language of celebration as well as sadness, of hope and humour as well as anger and despair. Grief is no respecter of persons, or propriety. The pain of loss is felt not only by lovers, by parents and children, but also by those who were never able to declare publicly either their love or their loss. Here we have the true voice of feeling, whether proper or private.

Hearts do break. Time passes, and as habit slowly helps to blunt the blade of loss you begin to recognise and learn to avoid the thoughts that lead in a downward spiral of sadness to despair; you also find out how to live with courage, and without self-pity. But none of it is easy. We hope you may find poems in this collection that will walk with you through the darkest and most difficult times, and help you to survive them.

We are grateful to the many distinguished poets who have offered their work for this anthology; we are equally grateful to those whose poems, though less poetically assured, deal with aspects of the subjects that no one else has covered, or who represent a particular personal situation; and to the young for their poems since loss is no respecter of age or of experience.

It is also our hope that as well as being interesting to any poetry reader, and a comfort in times of private mourning, the anthology will also be a source book, both inspirational and down-to-earth, for use at funerals, anniversaries, and memorials.

Shanta Acharya

REMEMBERING

After great pain, a formal feeling comes.
                                        Emily Dickinson

The more I try to forget the more I remember.

From now on I will accept ceremoniously
whatever thoughts come unbidden to me even in my sleep,
feelings that burst through the mists of my nervous forgetting,
memories of you that moisten my startled eyes as life's gifts.

When I listen to your CDs of Mozart, I will let the music
fill the infinite between our two souls. I will not try to measure
the extent of my loss in human terms. What good is there
in speculating about what-might-have-been?

I will not build a Pyramid or a Taj Mahal to our friendship
nor will I let the echoes of your words trapped in my limbs
haunt me like ghosts entombed in more formal relationships.
I will let the winds of change scatter my pain like ashes.

I will not change the locks to my heart, body or soul,
nor will I wait for your letter or phone-call.
I will be patient like a stone and let Time be my counsellor.
Perhaps, the less I try to forget the less I will remember.

SOMEWHERE, SOMETHING

We travel not to explore another country
but to return home fresh, bearing gifts.

Our lives the airports we fly from,
our bodies and souls, maps and compasses –

days the journeys we make,
past the continents we leave behind.

Surely there is somewhere, something
that justifies our coming and going?

Isn't that why we seek a sign from each other
of experiences worth dying for
as we commune with love under starlight
brittle with frost and the sharp taste of blood?

Let's fly free, not nailed to a mast;
see the universe with new eyes
not blinded by shadows that light casts.

Ann Alexander

DEATH IS A BIG WORD

Long and *lingering* are small words.
Kind is a small word, wishing it was a big word.
Cancer is a big word, one of the biggest,
but not as big as *death*.

Medicine is a small word.
Treatment is a tiny word, wishing it was a big word.
Hopeless, painful, these are small words.
You always and *you never*
are combinations of small words
which become big when used too often
and said with sufficient force.
See also *I love you* and *please don't go.*
If only and *too late* are small words

that become big words when said in a certain way.
Never is a big word. *Love* is a very big word
that will become small when used too often
and said without sufficient force.

Goodbye is a small word,
 except when used as a last word.

THE DWINDLING

When he died, after the initial tears, she enjoyed her busiest years.
Oh, the attention – faces she hadn't seen for half a lifetime
suddenly appeared. She had the cash – at last – to tart
the place up, depart for islands in the sun. But when
it was all done, the money spent, and the postman
forgot where she lived, Christmas came and
went, and the last friend died; the house
was sold, and she stopped going out,
for fear of the men – she shrank
into her bones and her clothes
seemed made for another
altogether as she sat
in the window
facing the
weather.
Oh, how
she missed
him then.

TO THE FRONT, AS NIGHT IS FALLING

Those who set up home by the sea
must consider the tides, and we do.
At the end of the day we walk to the sea, and talk
of the incoming, outgoing, neap and full,
high, ebb, spring and flood of the tides.

We consider the moon that sucks the tides;
full, horned, gibbous and pale,
waxing and waning, ringed and red.

The children, the ecstatic dogs,
louche youths under the granite walls,
have gone to earth.

Unobserved,
we sniff the wind that tickles the waves:
simoom, sirocco, willywar, breeze;
dip our squealing toes in the gravelly sea;
imagine the world that lies beneath –
its mountains and rifts, its wrecks, its bones;
the uplifting, collapsing of rock.

> Each morning he gets up,
> shakes his memory and the day to life –
> and if his eyes, his ears, his legs
> are every day a little less,
> the balance holds. Evening will come.

Walk me to the sea, he says then,
holding out his hand to save me from drowning.

Zeeba Ansari

WATER

You are no longer with me. You exist only
in rainy weather, in sedges, at the fringes
of clouds. Remember the river bank?
You stood, looking down, and said:
here in water's native land
words flow to the wadi of meetings —
your lifted finger stirred a crowd of gnats
to a second's world at sunset.
We held a ceremony for our dreams;
the last light presided; what we said
was heard by every living thing.

Your words were made of the air —
they passed through sunlight and could not last,
they were ghosts and passed over water
so could never rest. How was I to know
each word would be overlooked by silence?

★

This river has a guilty mind —
it remembers the time we lay at its side
and you showed me what comes
of picking the flowers. When I ask it to flow
now as it did then, it sits on its hands
and refuses to move. When you told me
somewhere in our lives we'd meet for good,
I believed you. How can I believe
the world as it is?

Forgive me this silence
you said, and wove your voice into the leaves —
I have closed the eyes of heaven to promise and fame
and sit like a swallow in the rain,
waiting for the spring to hear you again.

Sara-Jane Arbury

GRIEF

It woke me up this morning.
Naughty.
It knows it's not allowed on the bed.

Watched me all through breakfast.
Those hang-dog eyes.
No tit-bits. It'll get fat.

It keeps nudging me. Bumping its
nose against my knee. Once
it licked my hand.

I throw a stick to get rid of it.
But it brings it back, wanting more.
It won't leave me alone.

It teases me. Rolls over and
plays dead. Then gets up again.
Whines for attention.

I can't help stroking it.
Making a pet of it.
It owns me.

Could you resist it? Could you?
With its offer of love?
Limitless love?

Aileen Armitage – see Deric Longden

Alice Audsley

AT THE GATE

The crocuses crowd together
Unfolding their purple selves
As you lie folded
In your fourscore years.

Where are you
On this bright spring morning?
Do you feel the earthly warmth
Or see the boughs of the walnut tree
Shining in the sun?

In your stillness are you waiting
Like a prisoner at the gate?
Are you watching the distant
Dancing light of youth
The drops of gold
Amidst the certain uncertainty
Of your future now?

Is heaven greeting you?
Or bidding farewell
And setting you free?

R V Bailey

From *The Losing Game:*

(III) TRAVELLING IN THE DARK

It is 2 am. So intricately are you coiled
Around me that I scarcely breathe
In case you wake again to pain.

Statue-still through the waking night,
I follow the longest thought I know:
London. Stretching the legs of my mind,
I move along Kingsway, Fleet Street, Ludgate Hill;
Back to the Strand, to Embankment's
Wash of tides. Is it day or night
Here? Shall I take tube or bus?
London's tentacles reach out towards Essex,
Middlesex, Kent.

                    Here the church clock measures
Movement through dark, quartering silence,
As you breathe, in and out, in and out.
Each fourth breath pauses: long enough
For me to wish you might die here, now,
Gently, easily, in my arms. Ahead, Laocoön waits
To grasp you on some dreadful shore –
O why can't you die here, now, my love,
Just as I'm back from Hampstead,
Getting off the 134?

(IV) HANDS

In the old days, our hands met
Like fugitives, briefly, thrillingly,
By accident, at traffic lights, in the car.

Your hands, warm, light, dry
As newly-ironed sheets, fresh
As morning.

Your generous hands (ah –
When you poured the whisky!);
Your confiding hands, signalling
Clear as silent speech;
Your forgiving hands, impetuous
As applause, strong as all our love.

Your private hand in mine, or
Firm on the tiller, on the steering-wheel,
With the pen.
                    Now your hand
In mine's still warm, light, dry.
The tangle of tubes surrounding us
Drives you through your night, our night,
Offering no token that you know
I'm there. But then your grip was always
Gentle. We'll not lose touch.

(V) AT THE HOSPICE

Outside, the April grass is greener than grass.
Tranquil cows move over the meadow.
Walkers exercise dogs. Cars drive up,
Are parked, are driven away.

Inside, you lie under a sheet, obediently
Waiting for the shape-changer death
To move you on. *Sorry,* you say, as
Nurses tenderly turn you from side to side,
Sorry. I tell them you won't ring the bell,
Despite the pain: *We know,* they say. And later

I tell them you can't ring the bell at all. *Yes,*
They say. *We know.*

I feel I need respite care from myself,
You say. *Sorry.* And, near the end
Of all your meaningful words, *I am*
So dreadfully tired. Sorry.

Outside, light drains from the grass.
Inside, night and day, night and day,
Together we wait for the dark.
Sorry.

(VI) FINALS

Having set your foot on the threshold of eternity
At four am on Saturday, you're now
Establishing a world record for hesitation.

Day after day, night after night,
I wait with you, in this vestibule.
Fooled by my tenderness no longer,
You know that what you need's not me,
It's two young nurses, in sensible shoes,
With a syringe.

But I can't let you go: must focus on you, taut
Urgent, obsessed – you are my exam, and
This is Schools, Finals, the last day
Of the Tripos, the fatal minutes
Ticking by.

Despite my threadbare faith,
Somewhere inside it all your soul is safe.
If things were different, I know exactly
What you'd say to me –

Off with you, love! Enjoy it all –
I'll see you later.

(VIII) PARTS OF SPEECH

I must learn a new language: *I,* not *we;*
My, not *our.* Terms we never cared to use
Even in poems. But now, the only word
That's in my mind, day and night,
Night and day, is: *you.*

Of course, it is like falling in love.

Just as it was, forty-odd years ago,
You. The unimaginably marvellous
Had happened. It's called *you...you...you...*
Monotonous as pigeons. In my mind,
Night and day.
                Happily –
Though I guessed you'd pick up echoes –
No one else could hear this ground-bass to the
Rubbish (about Dickens, coffee, the use
Of the semi-colon) that my lips were on about.
You...you...you... though the coffee
And Dickens were holding their own
On the surface. A one-word thesaurus,
Me, with tunnel vision: *you.*

Dear ghost, you haunt me now as you did then,
As I wind the clock, feed the birds, distribute –
as you called it – the dishwasher fruit.
Now, as I drive, as I walk, landscapes
Dream their way past, unregarded
As Dickens and my colleagues years ago.
Insistent as logic, reliable as heartbeat,
Obsessive as any anorak spotting trains,
I'm still hooked. And it's still *you.*

(IX) HARD WORK

I think you liked me first for my hard work:
For doing things on time, and legibly.

I liked your laugh, subversive, sudden, rich
With possibilities of more to come, and how.

It wasn't industry or jokes: just love.
In time we dared to tell each other so.

And O my love, I'm still not one to shirk.
It's just I'm finding life without you now

Uncommonly hard work.

(VII) FAMILIAR

Call it unfortunate if you will – I
Can certainly understand why –
But love is so persistent. It just goes on
After, you might reasonably say, its usefulness is done,
However silent the house, empty the bed,
Obsequies long since over, long since buried the dead.

Love is a damaged thing, trailing absurd,
Forlorn and pathetic as a dressing-gown cord.
Intimate as breath, loyal as a shadow, close as a cry,
Nothing will shake it off.

                    Nor should you try.

TIDYING

How we'd relish talking about all this.
One day, together again, we'll find
The holiday side of nightmare.

I'm irrelevant here, yet I can't let go.
You'll never wake again, I know –
I'll not say: *Tea? I've brought us tea,*
As I used to, mornings after gigs,
Carefree on jumbo beds at anonymous inns
All over England.

Heart's the last thing going, and gallantly
Won't give up. The rest of you
Signed off days ago.

Your body's been out to get you
From the start: *If they're small as this*
We usually throw them back (the doctor,
The day you were born). Since then
It's been telling you, again and again,
How right he was.

These days, these nights: a tedious
Journey that at last leads home
To a broken home; where

Somehow fragments will have to be sorted,
Somehow assembled, somehow
Redeemed.

From time to time procedures must take place,
Which, they say, I shouldn't see. *(True:*
I have supped full of horrors already,
Watching your last night's fever.)
Meekly I leave, haunt corridors.
Find coffee.

★

The morning nurses have re-organised you,
Have left you, arms stretched on the sheet,
Something between Brueghel
And a tombstone knight. Your lower teeth
Gleam, strange in your mouth's gloom.
Can you not make her look – more at ease?

Ah sorry! It's a nursey thing, they say, *to be tidy.*
We'll turn her on her side.

Under the sheet, under
The crisp folds of the hospice sheet
Your hand's in mine. For my comfort,
Probably, warm, engaged as ever;
Yet maybe also for yours,
Who dreaming deep may need my hold
To steady you on your road.

My love, you are turning to
Compost now. Something, perhaps,
Good for roses, or poppies.

Time to move on to God.

★

Your breathing's bubble
And squeak drowns the April
Evening blackbird, will at last
Drown you. I pour a solitary *fino*
From the bottle we shared
While you still could swallow,
Toast your courage, your dear
Simplicity, your final
Leap into life.

Well-brought-up women don't cry. I tuck
The bits of my heart in my pocket,
Tidily; and remember I must
Say thank you to the nurse.

WITH YOU

I stand with you in the garden
The birds' surprising madrigals
Rise through the roar of bees.

I stand with you in the kitchen
Dear damaged long-loved over-used
Pans and pots protect us.

I stand with you in the hallway
With the deep oak tick of the clock
And the turning stair.

We sit by books in the lamplight
Importunate nondescript dog and cat
Surround us warmly.

We lie in the lofty bedroom
The church clock through the window
Quartering Gloucestershire silences.

Without you, no garden.
Sunshine withers on the plum tree
House shrinks derelict into dust.

Anne Ballard

DEAR DEPARTED

There's quite a turnout from his office:
that large white wreath came from them.
His coffin's ornate enough, not ostentatious.
The widow's new outfit, from Harrods,
sets off her rings well: she sniffs conscientiously.
The son drifts off into jetlag, stopped-over briefly
between New York and Dubai. The eulogy
is read by the barrister daughter –
confident at public speaking, wearing black
more naturally than the others.
Distant relations and in-laws
renew acquaintance, then forget each other
until the next time. The tasteful hymns
are chosen for familiarity. The vicar's
well briefed, advised to concentrate
on successful career and children…

… and nobody notices me:
the small dark woman with careless hair
who arrives late, slides quietly
into a back pew, kneels briefly,
bows her head, remains
slumped – dares not approach his grave
until the whole church has emptied.

HEARING THE NEWS

I was on the garden swing,
rocking gently, not to disturb
the mango cat purring beside me,
when they brought me the telephone.
Your son's voice: gave me the date, time,

then, when encouraged,
the details.

I had thought you were rallying
from his last report, assumed your reprieve
would outlast my holiday.

I hung up, saying nothing.
The words were like seeds
sinking deep, to rest in the dark.
I kept rocking.
The cat stretched, turned over:
through his toasted fur
I felt his heart beating.
The sun was warm.
Overhead, the tall trees
carried on turning.

THE STONE-RAISING CEREMONY

Black-clad, we congregate
like crows – a bone-chilled January day,
the synagogue colder grey granite.
At the entrance a square brass memorial
to six million dead.

The stone's testimonial
of his charm and weakness –
He never gave up on his dreams.
The wind gripes. Gravel and mud
wreck special-occasion shoes.

The Rabbi addresses the widow:
The past year's mourning is over;
how long and hard most of us know.

All year he has stood there in front of you
now he must move to your side,
to his rightful place,
and remain there
while you walk on.

She cried
as the ghost stepped aside.

Wanda Barford

CHATTERING

I'd love to phone you
and tell you what's been happening
over here – how I've cleaned
and tidied up your office
so you'd hardly recognise it
and thrown out eight bin-liners full;
how I haven't spent all your money
how I've rearranged the garden,
planted grass and a herbaceous border
to make it look more English, more like you;
how I've tried to project my voice
when reading, not to drop it
at the end of sentences; how your
five-year-old grandson often says:
Papa's dead, isn't he? as if trying
to make sense of *dead*; how we still
say grace before meals.

But here I go, I'm talking too much,
spending too long on the phone again.
Goodness knows what the cost will be
over such a long distance…

Judith Barrington

READY OR NOT

When is anyone ready to face the moon,
to stride up the dark avenue and look
into inevitable light? Some have turned back
babbling of the whiteness they saw there,
the dazzle at the threshold she guards.

> *I wasn't ready*, they say.
> *I had more to do,* they say.

One in a million will be granted the extension.
The rest of us go on wondering when she will call.
She is gleaming under a tree or behind
the inverted V of the green roof where rain putters,
each percussive drop a distraction from what must come.
When I've forgotten her altogether, she hops out
and locks onto my shoulder like an angry parrot.

> Her claws dig in.
> *I'm not ready*, I say.

SHOPPING FOR DEATH

We are searching for a spark
between the living and the dead –
something that might ignite near the carved name
that waits for a visitor,
one who perhaps has nothing left to say.

We are searching for a plot to buy – a plot
where the spark might catch
when one of us lies down there, bones intact
or maybe just a heap of ash – a flash
of recognition when the other appears

holding a flower from our garden
or a bowl of raspberries the dead one
is too dead to enjoy – eyes too empty
to appreciate the scarlet fruit
she once picked each morning before breakfast.

      I imagine myself the buried one.
      I imagine myself the visitor.

Visitor is easier to conjure
though more painful – loss being
an ache in the living body, an ache
I've felt before, whereas being the dead one
is unfathomable. Nothing at all like sleep.

Here is an available plot. A tree looms nearby.
Neighbours to the south, a close couple,
but somehow I don't warm to it
as if house-hunting on a street that fails to call out:

die here or *lie here* or *wait for someone to visit.*

We are searching for a spark between the living
and the soon-to-be-dead: one above, the other below
though we don't know which is which, don't know
upright from prone or what it will be like down there.
What if I should ask: *can I try it on for size?*

WHAT WE SAY

We say the tree is dead
        when leaves curl and crisp, spotted yellow
        or needles turn brown and fall to the ground
        leaving their branches naked.
We say the tree is dead
        when the trunk loses its sap

and one bare spar points to the sky
      pocked deep with the work of the woodpecker.
We say the tree is dead now
      when it falls like thunder
      tearing limbs from adjacent maples
      to stretch out its huge body on the earth.
Yes, we say, the tree is really dead
      as it softens there on the humus
      and saplings emerge from its hip, its barrel chest,
      well nursed as they talk back and grow leggy.
When is the tree ever dead? I say. Table? Beam?
      Window frame seen and touched, holding and held?
      We say we, too, are dead when breath and blood
      no longer rise, and limbs fail to move in the wind.
Lightning brings fire; burial slow rot,
      but scattered ashes are breathed in by strangers,
      graves visited, talked to, peed on by dogs –
      and stories are told of holding and being held.

Michael Bartholomew-Biggs

WIDOWER

Continuity
He knew they would be frightened of his feelings.
He could have worked it out
while they were scuttling up the motorway;
or in that extra time he had for thinking
as they failed to take the shortest route
to him across the city:
first the fruitless detour to the hospital
where he'd already left the empty-bedside;
then the corner shop
to pick up milk and thick-sliced Mother's Pride
they thought he might be short of.

He saw the car crawl up the hill and watched
them fumbling with the gate; then almost ran
to open up the front door wide
and admit their hesitation.
It's me, I'm still the same, he reassured them.

Surface reaction
The last thing that he saw her touch
was a cut-glass cruet.
Afterwards he searched its surface angles
for a fingerprint
to prove there was some corner
where identity persisted,
in loops indisputably her own.

Could he crystallize the essence
in this touch of tissue?
Or succeed in drawing out its spirals
like a spring to snare
the spirit of her double helix
and be less hellishly alone?

A dozen prisms
caught his speculation
and split it to its simplest colours,
whose names he would formerly have known.

Chaos
From far enough above no one can see
the jagged edges; fractals halve and fold
a finite coastline infinitely.
Boundary layers round events confine
each small disturbance hidden by streamlines
in incompressible and shock-free time.

It's been x months – that's all the neighbours know:
do they suppose that grass has grown on sorrow

like a seamless robe and made a sad slope
smooth enough to climb to get from then to now?
In fact, he's slid and scrambled daily for a purchase,
ignoring grit that's grazed his two hands' palms,
on the foreign cliff-face of her absence.

Heidi Beck

TELL GOOGLE SHE IS GONE
(i.m. Carolyn Jungr 1963-2007)

I searched for you today on Google
and you were there,
dining with the Swedish Ambassador,
making speeches in Montenegro,
as if you were still in residence,
chauffeured through the bombed-out streets
of Belgrade, rebuilding the world
with language and loans
and a certain force of will.

I can find pages of you
still working, still driven,
an engine of change,
but the search engine
fails to arrive at the place
on a pavement in Washington
where you fell
heart stopped
inexplicable
on your way home
for dinner.

INSTRUCTIONS FOR MY HEIRS

Do not put me in a box.
No gathered satin pinned with nails, no lid.
Let the coffin-maker starve.

I do not fear an endless night
laid out beneath retreating stars,
but not for me the claggy freight of soil.

Put me on a mountaintop, exposed
so wind can flay and shear my flesh.
Let microbes clear my bones until they clatter.

Or put me on a pyre, let me burn,
my vapours stretching for the stratosphere.
Let me be the dust that seeds the rain.

Find me in the air, the space,
the gaps between the pixels on this page.
I will be the oscillation,

the compression and release of waves.
Launch me. Let me sail.
Do not put me in a box.

Nikki Bennett

CLOTHES' MEMORIES

A grey suit with fitted jacket,
large buttons and a half-belt,
for a spring lunch in Chicago;
multi-coloured high-heels,
running for the bus in Düsseldorf;
lilac crocheted top,

for one evening in New York;
pale pink ballet pumps,
left behind once in a hotel;
midnight-blue fluffy robe
for early morning goodbyes;
boots for the winter,
bought near Ground Zero;
all packed away now
in a battered weekend bag;
charity shop gains,
by my loss –
my loss.

Judith Benson

THE SCENT OF HER

(i.m. my mother, Julia Searcy Lamar 1910-1996)

Suddenly, she's striding back into my life
as swiftly as she left, quick steps,
high heels on concrete, all bustle and chatter,
ordering me around, hands diving for my hair – *for heaven's sake*
can't you do something with that mop of yours?
Where did you get those tacky boots? You're not going out
with me looking like that. Gusts of wind, but mild,
that come bringing a shimmer of her whole person,
then gone again into *thin air.* There's nothing thin about air
when it becomes wind whisked off the roof.

Worse is the silence, when even my heart
doesn't speak to me, something dead inside,
living in a minus dimension in the key of flat,
all stoppered up, can't smell a thing,
can't remember the scent of that *Le Bleu*

she had to have from every Duty Free,
her face going all funny to say those two French words,
Le Bleu. The way it sometimes is without her.

COLUMBARIUM

(i.m. my father Captain 'Rags' Parish 1905-1995)

It's the misunderstanding of ashes at the airport,
confusion over containers at the Academy,
the solemnity, the familiar uniform;
it's the gun salute sending shock waves across the water,
the bugle playing Taps,
the presentation of the flag,
the young cadet's voice trembling;
it's the smooth leaded box slotted in,
sun glint on engraved wings,
the miniature blue and gold curtains closing
that is our undoing.
We unravel in the wind,
so many bits of string without a kite.

Zanna Beswick

ALWAYS

Sometimes the night brings him in
in the fold of a fox's bark
or the eager wailing of cats.
And you are sitting by the fireside
where the coals pursue their private Etna,
country of molten caverns,
the lava dragons shifting in their lair.
The pages of your book lie open,

the thronged words running on without you –
lives to be lived and fought out by chapter –
independent of attention.
You have your own stories dreaming themselves
in the rich tresses of memory,
all the tones of hope, anxiety, laughter, discontents,
the palpable skein of what love is.

You turn to meet its glance.

And night has brought him in.
The chair is empty,
the quiet hearth settled.
Yet just beyond sight
he stands in the silence where touch was,
enfolds you in the wings of rest.
Later will come the sharp tang of dawn;
stars fall to brighten grass,
the chattering pigeons, the early-rising pheasant.
Still lingers the embrace,
unspoken now, transcendent.

Elizabeth Birchall

PARCELLING UP THE CRUCIFIX

The will is the easy part – disposal
Of clothes to a charity shop,
Furniture to any house-clearer, the few
Treasures or books and records to each of you
According to your interests, with love.

The hardest part is
Their unread books, their unsaid prayers,

Purposes you cannot share; you betray
Yourself as well as the dead
Even as you seek to satisfy.

The missal and the crucifix –
The rubbish bin's unthinkable
And yet their potency lies only
In that life you cannot live or resurrect
But must treasure and respect.

Vivienne Blake

DIMINUENDO

Clashing chords of breakers on remote rocks
welcome ghosts from her past to the island.
Among them, a stranger stands by the shore;
her crashing glissando of tears declares
the despair of a cellist unable to play.
Hidden, the glory of not making music –
no matter. The sound that surrounds her
is one with gannets, puffins and terns,
a sweeter, more raucous concerto.
Musician's mastery,
too soon gone,
diminishes,
dwindles,
calando,
calm.

Patrick Bond

WATCHING FIREWORKS WITHOUT YOU

I never meant to miss you so much,
I did not know I could fall so far.
Standing in the cool blue and pink of waking,
Hearing the torn cry of the seagull.

I did not know how dark, how velvet and deep,
The falling, as I watched bright stars that night
Rise, the silver-fluted columns of fire, the ruby rain,
The knowing I could not catch you, or hold the night for you.

I did not know your face, in photographs, in the fog of years,
Would pull and pull, that the gravity of eyes
So arrowed in time, so centred, so love-formed, would pull
My heart, crying, out of me into the falling dark.

Pat Boran

OBITUARY

His heart had four chambers where turf smoke tumbled.
His eyes filled with sky, like the pools in the yard.
His feet were the stones you hit with a shovel
when digging potatoes. His shoulders were hard.

He was the uncle we seldom encountered,
my father's reflection going unseen
between cow shed and creamery. His love, unexpected,
moved with the slow step of a man in a dream:

a dream among animals, a dream under stars,
a dream with, at best, two or three songs to name it,

a pint the odd evening, what passed for a car,
a few biscuits, the transistor, his bachelor gamut
of feelings expressed in the bark of his dog,
wind through the hayloft, those fields under fog.

WINTER BURIAL
(i.m. Liam Brady)

Twin jet trails crossing the sky;
here's us frozen in the lake of time
and up there God goes blithely skating by.

LET'S DIE

Let's die, I say to my kids,
Lee aged five, Luca not yet three,
and under an August blanket of sun
we stretch out in the grass on a hill
to listen to the sea just below
drawing close, pulling back,
or to the sheep all around us
crunching their way down towards earth.

Do you love the clouds, Dada?
Do you love the Pink Panther?
and *Will you stay with us for ever?*
to which I reply, without hesitation,
Yes, Yes and *Yes* again,
knowing that as long as we lie here
everything is possible, that any of the paths
up ahead might lead us anywhere
but still, just in time, back home.

Like me, sometimes they act too much,
filling the available space and time
with fuss and noise and argument,
but up here, overlooking the landscape,
the seascape, of their lives, on this hill
they like to play this game, to lie
together and together to die
which, in their children's language, means
less to expire or to cease
than to switch to Super Attention Mode,
to prepare for travel, to strap oneself
into the booster seat and wait and wait
for the gradual but inexorable lift
up and off and out into motion.

For my two boys, things are only
recently made flesh, made mortal –
our uprooted palm tree, two goldfish,
the bird a neighbour's cat brought down
last week – and they are almost holy
with this knowledge. *Let's die now,*
then let's go home for tea, Lee says,
putting into words as best he can
the sea's helpless love affair with the land.

Pat Borthwick

CHAIR

A broken chair
leant against the allotment shed
casts its own row of shadows.
A widow will read them
in a different way to the child
who sees a line of animals,
waves rolling across the bay,
the gentle slopes of Grandad's sheets
before he left that Wednesday night.
They said he'd gone to visit somebody
whose name sounded as if it started with 'J'
like jelly and Grandad's geraniums.
There are times even a child knows
that some questions
must remain inside their head.
The plot grows thicker than a jungle.
There will be a season
when a broken chair,
propped against the leaning shed,
takes root, comes into leaf. Possibly
a flower or two.

THE WASH

Father, forgive us for finding you out this way,
your three children undressing you
to look like Mammy's plucked goose lying there.
How you'd hate us to see this naked truth
preferring your weather-hardened coat
buttoned to the chin, your tight-laced boots,
your pulled-down cap.
We are charged with the task of bathing you

before the delicacy of your shroud,
your skin suddenly our own skin.
   We are amazed to find we even share
the same imperfections of our feet –
toes three and four like Siamese twins.
I'm soaping them while Michael wipes
what he says is a tear from your eye.
   You always told us that to cry
was a breached dam or broken fence
the herd could wander through.
        And when Colm
shook out your pockets just now
instead of knives and baler twine,
there were sacks of seed.
   And was that a lake,
a full sun swimming in it?
   Your crumpled handkerchief
contained a shower of moths and butterflies
enough to fan the whole Earth
into a different orbit, or further.
       And then Father,
from deeper in your pocket,
a nest enclosing three warm and freckled eggs.

Stephen Boyce

STONES
(i.m. DB)

I nearly went arse over tip on the footpath to Lundy Bay
where violets, primrose and spring squill were jostling
in the last of the sun with scurvy grass and speedwell;

I clambered over the boulders, with half an eye on the tide
that sucked and slopped in the hollows, as I looked for pretties
and paperweights – for stones are a comfort in sorrow.

And I turned up granite and quartz, flat skimmers of shale,
limestone smoothed by the ebb and flow, and a slew
of coppery pebbles tumbling down to the foam;

then heaved myself back up the cliff, pockets bulging with rocks,
as a stonechat sang in the tangled gorse and alder swayed
in the wind, while the boats out at sea held their course.

So I bring you nothing but stones and I let these stones
speak for me, that hold their own in the storm, keep faith
with the tide and the land; for we measure in millions
the years they have been here, and the years till they turn to sand.

Sue Boyle

WIDOW

The week her husband,
my father, died
my mother walked

to Ryman's the stationers
half way down the High Street
on the left hand side
and bought a special offer
paper shredder
which she carried home
boxed though it was and bulky
along the over-arching lime walk
where the trees were already
surrendering
their sour confetti of yellow green
and began to shred his papers
all sixty hoarded
box-filed years of them.
It took her almost a month.
I have four years left, she said.
I am going to live my life.

THINKING ABOUT THE SWANS

Colour is a lesser thing than light:
no bird's gaudy can compete with the white
of swans. Absorbed in their own loveliness
they glide as if they knew a world more fine
than this, their heads inclined
not in the search for food but in a kind
of graceful prayer. Those who paint angels choose
to wing them like swans as if to prove
how close and familiar heaven is
but there is a colder thought –
like white swans flying into falling snow
our dead abandon us; their wingbeats grow
fainter, then vanish. They become
part of the sky's thick silence and are gone.

AT THE HOSPITAL

It is our turn today.
Our friends are kind
but glad
as if this thing
can only happen
in any one house
on any one given day.

They feel more safe
because more safe than us
savour their happiness
because we are here
because we are at this pass
are more aware of clocks
how light diminishes
from zenith to the last
of the precious day.

Their talk is gentle
they remember making love
take out their photographs
what lovely things have been
tidy their houses more
tenderly than usual
for the night.

We are deep voyagers to them
already on our way
to a distant world.
A nurse brings tea in a fat mug
two shortbread biscuits
wrapped in cellophane
and checks your drip.
She knows, our friends know.
Everybody knows.

Alison Brackenbury

THEN

When death stalks, do not bring me pale carnations,
or heavy roses children crouched to spray
in plastic tunnels. Open the stiff window,
although the air is fresh and smells of night.
If it is July, I will hear swifts,
their restless rage, their flickered, furious flight.

AFTERMATH

I cleaned two homes. I learnt one thing.
What will survive of us is not
our careful words, our gardens' grace,
but rubber bands; green balls of string.

FOR THE NEW YEAR

She was delighted by the sudden gift
after thirty years. How old must he be?
She had seen one shot, the skin still beautiful,
while her face carried the sorrows of the world
below her eyes. No, better not to meet,
reply discreetly. Why had he sent it now?
Safety in numbers? Flutters in the heart?
It was good (she told herself) not to be young,
not to bear that unending sadness, hope.
The sun was frowning before massive storms.
She stowed the gift. She kept the envelope.

2 a.m.

Then, when she woke,
she did not know if she was young.
But her coffee was cold
and everyone had gone.

Sarah J Bryson

TIME DELAY

On the dresser his ashes
wait for her final decision.

She sits alone with the newspaper.
Sounds drift in, so the blackbird's song

in the cherry tree and the click
of the window caught in the breeze

mix with the tick of the clock
and the rev of a car as it pulls away.

The cat stretches and moves
from floor to chair to follow the shaft of sun

her tortoiseshell coat flecked with gold.
The radio in the kitchen relays Big Ben

and the newsprint blurs, unreadable now
as the day fades.

Denise Bundred

FOETAL SCAN

They're laughing at a private joke. Her blouse glides
a pattern of tiny flowers across her rounded belly.
He should be at school. Not sitting here in holey jeans,
stretched brown T-shirt, love-bite purple on his neck.

I spread cold gel across warm skin. You turn,
show me your heart beating beneath my hand.
I see the twisted valve, the missing chamber. Your heart,
the same size as the tiny fist gesturing me away.

Leave me alone. Don't tell my parents yet.
When you breathe, after that perilous journey
into light, your heart will falter and fail.
For a few minutes more, they think you are perfect.

BREAKING THE NEWS

I bend and listen, stethoscope on grey skin.
Blue ships on the curtain. Monitor's rhythm stumbles.
You watch your child, and hope.

We'll speak in the Quiet Room. Come with me.
This door here. No, after you. Please
be seated. Are you comfortable?

The room is small and cold, white walls
no windows. Sofa too low, not enough chairs.
Pink silk roses on a table marked by coffee cups

and a telephone for after.
I speak slow, solemn words. When you ask
to know the truth, you want me to lie.

WEIGHING WORDS

She weighs words like morphine calculated to a tenth
of a milligram, or a diamond measured to quarter of a carat;
She balances words like the pawnbroker, weighing a couple
of bracelets, a broken necklace and a wedding ring.
She feels the weight of words in the air of the room
lightens or darkens them to where they need to be.

> It is her place to impart information
> which spills beyond words, suggests more
> than the sum of all their vowels and consonants.

She weaves words fine as linen, chooses them
like silk thread selected to sew bright letters
on a sampler that was never finished.
She blends words like the *chocolatier*
to just the right degree of sharpness, offers
the mixture as sweet or bitter as it must be.

> Her words probe like the fingertips which palpate
> your husband's chest as he lies in the shade
> of the night-light on Bailey Ward.

She measures the space between words in nanoseconds
too short and you may not feel their full significance, a train
at speed and you can't read the names on station platforms;
too long and the time between them swells
like the cupboard in the bedroom when you were a child
and you attribute more than she intends.

> She searches for words which catch you as you fall
> a net or lifebelt in the storm, but sometimes
> only a hand is enough, to hold tight to.

She has used these words before (will do so again)
but each time she shapes them differently.

And if you have no questions left to ask,
she has done all she could. Yet she bends
under failure's weight when she must say
I'm sorry, there is no more we can do.

MOTHERHOOD

The operation is taking longer
than expected.
I carry this message to his mother
who swallows cold tea
hungry for news.
Doing everything they can,
doesn't seem enough.

Spot-lit in Intensive Care
her seven year old lies still
beneath the white sheet.
I sit beside her as we will
his oxygen saturation up,
hope his heart rate down
even a little.

Don't focus on a single number
We must take the picture as a whole.
The whole picture is crumbling.
Knowing more than her, knowing
nothing more will help,
I interrogate the charts.

The surgeon shakes his head.
The intensivist cannot pull
a single soft white rabbit
from his hat.

Alarm announces a faltering rhythm
this time falls and falls again.
Other monitors join the dissonance of sound.
We persist for thirty minutes
and another ten.

I'm so sorry but he's gone.
I am buffeted by the tumult
of her pain. We sit nursing
teacups as the sun rises outside
that windowless room.

I drive home, enter the silent house
kiss my seven year old son awake.

Elizabeth Burns

THE ARRIVAL

I dream that the woman in the horse-drawn cart
is being pulled into a dark lake flecked with stars,
but she's ready to go, she lets the horse lead her

deep into that cold, enfolding water and those of us
who watch her go speak one word: *advent.*
I wake to the sound of the phone and the news

of your death in the night. Later, as instructed
in the dream, I look up the meaning of the word
and find *a coming, an arrival.*

David Burridge

ON A NEED-TO-KNOW BASIS

There is the wait of course, like holding a high note,
not knowing when to breathe. Jaw set to a fixed bite,
finger rubbing plastered sting. Occasional wheelchair bang,
doors swing open, white coats appear, murmur and vanish again.

I strut in my head – want it all squared – being a man of facts.
But behind curtains and screens they know more than me.
So stare at the wall in this wobble of time,
afraid of just what they can see.

We are ushered into a quiet space – I should sit at ease –
tea is an option but that would sentence me. I remember
the sip preceding my Mother's dying news.

In a fashioned moment I am part of a team chat;
the focus is on me without the need to rib-dig.
Everybody is at hand; they know the steps down,
feed me information as if a tube had been slipped in.

A random mutation nothing I could have done.
Would have preferred a bit of divine judgement –
the chance to argue my case. I make a joke
about the man smoking at the door.
We all laugh and move on.

Robbie Burton

WALNUT

What we need to do, you and I,
is imagine ourselves inside a walnut

where a tough skin holds us apart
but we're still two halves of a whole.

We'll forget that one half will wither,
and work hard to ignore

the other half, out of the shell,
being complete.

IT TAKES MORE THAN A WAVING HAND

For instance, boats.
I tried saying goodbye to one of those.
To its burbling propeller and ticking kettle.
To the doily of sunlight patched above our bed.

Goodbye, I said, marking danger points
on my mind's eye map. Trunk roads crossing
hump-back bridges. Marinas squaring up
to the west coast mainline.

But people giving lifts don't follow my rules.
They take roads past sudden canals where
lovers still chat on narrow boat roofs
and fall asleep later in firelight.

Some things won't be said *goodbye* to.

GLOSE: OPEN SPACE

You'd think that in all this open space,
nothing but fields for miles around
and some cows and trees, you'd get a signal.

(from *Signal*, Mimi Khalvati)

And let's not forget the prayer tree.
Not that I've hung it with his sheet music
or old ties – just climbed the rabbit track
to settle against a branch at leaning level.
Easy to find solitude up here.
You'd think that. In all this open space.

Usually, it's larks that surprise. Once
it was a dead twig dropping from the sky.
Can buzzards catch the edge of such
a falling? I have this and other questions.
Better to ask out loud with
nothing but fields for miles around.

I've given God and my late husband
every chance. A sycamore leaf
falling on my shoulder would be nice.
Or words (not mine) arriving in my head.
You'd think by praying among larks
and some cows and trees, you'd get a signal.

Maggie Butt

ADDRESS BOOK

Here names hide in the leaves
like scorpions, ambush you unawares
in the middle of the morning. Names
which scorch, their voices silent.
And what to do? Ink out?
Obliterate? The violence of night.
A truth too far.

Tippex would cover them as graves
in snow, a bump of scar tissue
reminding of the wound it hides.
A simple cross then, furled white sails
of evening, beyond which the name
remains, glimpsed as through a gate,
which opens to another time, another world.

THIS IS HOW THE GENERATIONS PULL APART

My daughter's hand is dragged from mine
by the weight and press of commuters
on the Moscow underground – heedless,
uncaring of her smallness and my panic
as the doors close between us.

Now mum drifts in and out of sleep,
in and out of herself, her hand slipping
from mine in slow motion. No knowing
if there's a station further down the line
where she might watch for me.

ICE RINK

Four years.
And now the cavernous well
which yawned inside
has become so familiar
that I can skirt around
its slippery-scree edges
with confident, easy steps.

Slowly I have papered over
the beckoning blackness
(*don't look down!*)
with strips of translucent tissue paper;
building layer upon layer
into a *papier mache* ice rink
crisp as an egg shell,
which one day
may be strong enough to bear my weight.

GO GENTLE

Why not go gentle into that good night
like drifting into sleep from sun-soaked day,
remembering the brightness of the light?

Weary of gross indignities, take flight,
wave off the drugs, dementia, slow decay,
why not go gentle into that good night?

Good housewives, who have polished fiercely bright
both floors and faces, earned this holiday
remembering the brightness of the light.

Wild women who could drink and dance all night
flop down and kick your achy shoes away,
why not go gentle into that good night?

73

Grave women, who face death with failing sight
let memory fling you back from this cold clay
remembering the brightness of the light.

And you my mother, there on the sad height,
dive cleanly from your tower of fear, I pray.
Why not go gentle into that good night,
remembering the brightness of the light?

Richard Carder

BENEDICTION

(Lines written a few furlongs above Tintern Abbey, August 1996)

After a day of walking with melancholy,
Haunted by memory of your pain,
Endured grimly to a bitter end.
Light began to fade.
I turned to climb the hill tent-wards
Through the wood; the path after rain
Scrunched stonily; balsam stalks rose
Head-high, or leaned dusky pink flowers
Across the track.
           Suddenly, a scuffle
In the bushes, and bursting before me
Greyly, a badger on the path,
Lurching and sniffing ahead,
Oblivious of my presence.
I stopped, entranced. Another ran out
From under a hazel, a young cub
Playfully scuffling this way and that,
Then darting back into green thicket,
A benediction of badgers!
I followed carefully, quiet as I could be,

Until she spied me and shot off to the side
And safety under canopy of leaves.
My heart lightened and lifted,
Emerging at the top to scattered red clouds
In the dim blue sky of a vast horizon.

Jennie Carr

EDGE TREE

The rain is clearing, a tough
breeze pulls the clouds apart.
With weighted backpack we climb
steadily towards the ridge
heather scratching at our toecaps.
At the crest we walk its back
following the dry stone wall.

When we reach the weathered place
we have no words; the plastic urn
is hastily opened, shaken
vigorously side to side,
its copious contents strewn
to a wind that tugs at the tree
spirals her ash away in ribbons.

You can see it from her kitchen window
while you fill the kettle at the sink,
the last one crouching on its own
along the sky-lined edge.

UNTITLED

No one knows
why some don't belong,
the one who tails me
is always alone

my at-a-distance companion
outcast of my pedestrian day;
his solitary shadow slips
through trees and streetlights

shifts across supermarket aisles
and office doors.
His huge paws pad
my borders.

He chooses the dark hours
to cross them.
I hear a snuffle at the window
a half-keening whimper

so unbearable
I let him in.
His big nose nudges
my aching throat

his breath
is my breath;
I tilt back my head
and howl.

Caroline Carver

He's clinging to a drawer from the chest in his cabin
and because he hasn't slept in 36 hours
it's the only thing that keeps him afloat

his mind fogs with smoke   he imagines
it's his wife he holds in his arms
in the seductively warm Mediterranean sea

and perhaps in the drawer
instead of the water that keeps overwhelming it
he's guarding their child

a child with a precocious memory   who will never forget
the rough man-smell of his jacket
the pipe stuffed awkwardly into his pocket

All round him   in a sea roughened by battle
men are dying   only a few
out of more than 800 will reach the shores of Crete

A rating floats near him
holding on to nothing more than a wooden plank
and weeping   because one small thing

small in the terrible significance of war
has finally cut him down
he's lost his special charges   the ship's dog and cat

None of them should ever have been sent into battle
after three actions in quick succession
and nearly all ammunition gone before they started

by the end they were firing dummy bullets
against the Stukas who are still bombing the waters around them
the enemy who – so surprisingly – came from the air

A sailor weeps   his commander holds onto a floating drawer
mind going back to another May   in England
when he's swimming in a river

because his mother-in-law has ordered him there
to retrieve the cups he threw overboard from the galley
of the family houseboat   and he remembers

how his wife loved him in his uniform   how proud he was
as he stood in the bow of his brand-new ship
how joyfully he threw his young daughter up in the air

Rosalie Challis

HEBE

They wrapped you in your old grey rug
to take you from this house.

Now you have come back to us,
your fur soft as ash.

You will join your calm shadow
beside the bench on our lawn

and the fig-tree's deep shade
where you lay at summer's height.

We will glimpse your head, its fine
curve the shape of the human hand,

let the garden remind us of the bond
which binds man and dog,

as we move from morning sun
to the peace of dust to dust.

Gillian Clarke

ON THE TRAIN

Cradled through England between flooded fields
rocking, rocking the rails, my head-phones on,
the black box of my Walkman on the table.
Hot tea trembles in its plastic cup.
I'm thinking of you waking in our bed
thinking of me on the train. Too soon to phone.

The radio speaks in the suburbs, in commuter towns,
in cars unloading children at school gates,
is silenced in dark parkways down the line
before locks click and footprints track the frost
and trains slide out of stations in the dawn
dreaming their way towards the blazing bone-ship.

The Vodaphone you are calling
may have been switched off.
Please call later. And calling later,
calling later their phones ring in the rubble
and in the rubble of suburban kitchens
the wolves howl into silent telephones.

I phone. No answer. Where are you now?
The train moves homeward through the morning.
Tonight I'll be home safe, but talk to me, please.
Pick up the phone. Today I'm tolerant
of mobiles. Let them say it. I'll say it too.
Darling, I'm on the train.

A DEATH IN THE VILLAGE

The lanes are under snow of the thorn
and weighted with chains of wild laburnum
and nothing's different about the day,
except for the 'never again' death speaks.

We stop at the next farm to share the news
with our neighbour. 'A lovely man.'
For a while he's at the heart
of our talk and our silence

when everything shifts a bit –
a widow, a farm, a funeral,
his workshop where at this moment
sunlight is casting a dust-sheet

over oil guns, solder, an old lathe,
the things an engineer keeps, in case,
the secrets of a man and a shed,
its seemly disorder and grace.

Only last week, bringing us tools,
he stepped in to admire the joinery
in our new room, and spoke of a carpenter
he knew, suddenly, shockingly dead.

You never know, he will always say
when it's summer again and the kite flaunts
above the may-trees and golden chain,
what is before you.

Rachael Clyne

TERMINAL CONVERSATION

What can we talk about when
events in the rest of the house
no longer hold meaning

when tomorrow really is
a singular possibility
and the outside world
or any future stops
at this room?

What can I say when
everything I mention
points to your departure?

Tending your body
bathing in silence together:

the only conversation left.

TIDYING DRAWERS

At last finding space to tidy
she adjusts the drawers
to sit flush with the chest
at the same time her life –
the semblance of control.

>   Closing the crack in the fabric
>   of her world, the departure
>   so sudden; its aftershocks
>   of lost purse and power-cuts
>   now subsiding.

It is comforting to know
how a drawer is held
together by dovetails,
so it slides easily back
into the cavern of a chest.

Claire Coleman

ONE WAY

One way of being intimate with the dead
is to wear clothes they have given you.

Slip on the person you are missing;
over and over put on your mother.

It's what we spurn that haunts us;
no returns, no second chances.

What matters most?
Touch the gifts you have,

hold them close. Choose
this cotton top she gave you from East,

this pure wool jumper from Marks and Sparks,
wear a pair of socks with multi-coloured hearts;

layer over layer, cover yourself in love.

NOVEMBER WINDOW

I appear to be going just fine
in low gear or neutral.
Stop-start traffic
past humdrum country hedges.
Then, sudden red
in the hedgerow. Bryony;
bright scarlet drops twined
round and down bitter sloe stems.
Three months since the funeral.
I appear to be coping just fine
in low gear or neutral,
but sudden as the sudden
falling red, my own heart's
stalling, stalling.

David Cooke

ROUTINES

The simplest routines can save us, the phone call
a daughter makes each morning at nine o'clock
in which the words are nothing but tokens
worn to a sliver; or small change so valueless
you'd wonder why it's minted.
                                                    But then,
like nothing else, the routine alerts us
when the call's unanswered and we try again
and then once more, knowing the silence
can be explained by a short walk
to the paper shop, or a problem with his stoma,
that stops him picking up, while just in case
we cross town through fixated traffic

to where he's beached on soiled sheets,
hapless and alone.
                    Through a night
of whispering, of resignation and last rites,
his daughter keeps her vigil
until he blinks and then returns,
from wherever, alive at his own wake,
flirting outrageously with his nurses,
and wondering slyly if by chance
he'd be OK for a *Guinness*.

CHEMO

The six months they gave you and which,
in no time, became a year
are stretching out into another.

It seems that minutes and hours
are made of stubborn stuff. They are filled
with nonsense that keeps you going –

your repertoire of dud jokes
or the crazy hat you wore all winter
to show the world you hadn't gone.

The chemo chases through your system,
erupting here and there: your blistered throat
so raw, it quietens you for days;

the scurf that scalds
your face. You have shucked off
loosened toenails

and hold out your fingertips.
They are blank, abraded. You claim defiantly
that now the cops can't trace you.

Annemarie Cooper

JET EARRINGS

This is how her mother mourned,
below her pale scraped-back hair
black mirrors clipped to each ear.

The child said they were listeners
for in case he could come near.

After the funeral the black two-piece
and the hat with the veil were put away
but not the jet earrings.

They weighted her mother's ears
for three years more.

Until, said the child, her mother was sure
wherever he was it was too far.

Wendy Cope

DUTCH PORTRAITS

To find myself in tears is a surprise –
Paintings don't often get to me like this:
These faces with their vulnerable eyes
And lips so soft that they invite a kiss;
The long-haired husband, gazing at his bride
With evident desire, his hand around
Her wrist, six years before she died –
Both so alive and so long underground.
And here's a husband who resembles you
When you were plump and bearded. It's too much.
He looks so happy and his wife does too,
Still smiling, now they can no longer touch.
Someone will read our story, by and by.
Perhaps they'll feel like this. Perhaps they'll cry.

SPARED

That Love is all there is,
is all we know of Love...
                    Emily Dickinson

It wasn't you, it wasn't me,
Up there, two thousand feet above
A New York street. We're safe and free,
A little while, to live and love,

Imagining what might have been –
The phone-call from the blazing tower,
A last farewell on the machine,
While someone sleeps another hour,

Or worse, perhaps, to say goodbye
And listen to each other's pain,

Send helpless love across the sky,
Knowing we'll never meet again,

Or jump together, hand in hand,
To certain death. Spared all of this
For now, how well I understand
That love is all, is all there is.

THE WIDOW

(from *'The Audience': poems commissioned by
the Endellion String Quartet*)

I like this piece. I think you'd like it too.
We didn't very often disagree
Back in the days when I sat here with you
And knew that you were coming home with me.
This is the future. It arrived so fast.
When we were young it seemed so far away.
Our years together vanished like a day
At nightfall, sealed forever in the past.
I can't give up on music, just discard
The interest we shared because you died.
And so I come to concerts. But it's hard.
Tonight I'm doing well. I haven't cried.
My head aches. There's a tightness in my throat.
And you will never hear another note.

Kay Cotton

PASSPORT

You don't need a passport to get to Heaven

I won't put it on the wicker coffin, under your purple sunhat,
the one with a leather thong and a scarab bead.

A TREAT AND A SCRABBLE

You paid for my spider crab,
my whelks, three oysters.
The taste of them passes
faster than the smell of the sea
under my thumb nail.
The evening breeze brings in
a tidal sound and thought
of those thin boys by the Dockyard wall
jumping into mud up to their necks
for small coin, as I am, in the rising loss
of what you used to be,
left with a Scrabble game
I cannot lose, the game
you cannot win.

REGISTRATION INK

Registration ink darkens with age.
It has no acidic qualities, doesn't eat the paper.

The certificate has no mention of Seaham,
there's nothing in the sub-district of Easington
to signify the coal-dust on the stones of the beach,
the 'best dress' Christmas parties at the Big House.

No copperplate hand describes your occupations;
the first one to create a School Library System,
driving books through all the seasons of Hampshire.
'Chief Children's Librarian' doesn't cover it.

No copperplate signature over the One Penny Stamp
with the head of the Sovereign in a wreath of laurels
marks the occasion of your passing,
the timeliness, discretion, the quietness of it.

Watermarks are there: The Imperial State Crown,
heraldic flowers, entwined leaves pressed into thin
paper trying to be vellum. This can't encompass
a poet's imagination. The print hammers you down.

Registration ink darkens with age.

Martyn Crucefix

'BY THE MID-DAY SUN'

We tramp up the garden
over sodden slippy grass
to three silver birches that mark the boundary

and someone might see us
bringing fork and spade
and this black bin liner to the foot of the trees

where we eye mossy cushions
and gravitate to this
barely visible mound where you point and speak –

somebody might see us
as I slice open the earth
complicated by roots but in this precise spot

the spade slides in well
as if re-opening a hole
and someone might watch as you crouch and scrape

your fingers staining dark
as you rake back the soil
and I thrust in the fork – someone might catch us

now both on our knees
like archaeologists
unearthing an object the size of a sweet jar

but maroon in colour
and punctured by my fork
and you take it to wrap in the black bin liner

then stand to wait
as I shovel the soil
into the scar of the hole that moss will soon cover –

and somebody might gaze
on our little *cortege*
herded back to the house your mother warmed

and dressed all those years
now she's a little mixed
with its beloved soil as each step confirms

possession is temporary
even a place of rest
you lean against the car you begin to let go

'WISH'D FOR THE MOON'

In New Year's cold
of yesterday's white dawn
I opened the boot
of your old blue car
to gifts your daughter
bought doctors and nurses

in confident anticipation
in those brighter days
just before Christmas

of the hour approaching
when you'd no longer
depend on their attention

would emerge blinking
into New Year's dazzle
its expanses of blue
after the airless space
of the filthy ward
leaning hard on the arm

of your grateful husband
your dark-haired daughter
who tonight is shaking
beside me in bed
tears raw as earth-tremors
each one too fierce

for whatever I can offer
in such a poor return –
till we each lie breathing
in dread of February
its sheets of snow
transforming the nature

of cars on the street
these gifts of chocolate
and sweet perfumed soap
one bottle of fire-
hot brandy grown cold
with the hours and more

dense with the cold
left untouched still
in the boot of your car
its amber dead-weight
like Spring itself
sprawled stiff in its bed

Tim Cunningham

LOSING HIS GRIP

Today his world is flat
And he lies flat
At the edge of the cliff,
Stretched taut,
Tortured on the rack

Of her slipping away,
Fingers losing their grip
And her frantic
Feet dangling
Like a hanged man's,

One shoe fallen
On the rocks below.
Nothing hurts more
Than this holding on,
Nothing, except the letting go.

BEYOND THE WOODS

When I am gone, I will leave
A Hansel and Gretel trail
Across the stepping-stone stars.

Follow them. Find me.
Or how can that place
Be called heaven?

NOT BEING THERE

I still remember you not being there
That August at the chapel's wrought-iron gate
When the birds' *schola cantorum* intoned vespers
And my role was to check the time and wait.

We planned to walk by Guinness' canal,
Content to be together in the sun.
But I learned on that solitary stroll
That ultimately each one walks alone.

Your mother unexpectedly took ill
And there was no way you could let me know
That evening when our paths diverged, and still
I see the bulrushes, the dusty stones.

This time it's not your mother who is unwell,
And the pallbearers are always punctual.

WOMAN MUCH MISSED
(Thomas Hardy's *The Voice*)

You are missed
By the hall's morning mirror
Framing your reflection
As you rush for the bus,
By birthday candles and balloons
Waiting for your breath,
By *Wuthering Heights* and *Emma*
Without your eye
To dance across the page,

Much missed by the primrose
Blossoming without your sudden praise,
By March's mischievous fingers

That used to tousle your hair,
The blackbird disappointed
By your absence in the stalls,

And missed most by the hand
Still reaching out to touch your hand
Knowing it is not there.

CHILD ALARM

You came home early in that wooden box.
A sudden ending to your holiday.
Sudden as the out-of-nowhere car
That flashed like some conductor's baton

Knocking your song right out of key
And opening doors I cannot enter. I was not there,
But for mothers the impossible is no excuse.
My arms ache now with the weight of emptiness,

Clutch at memories. Religion's good news
Is lost in the post. Philosophy brings
Only the idea of consolation. But I keep
The child alarm switched on and listen

As you lie cradled in eternity,
Reassured you are not crying in your sleep.

Julia Darling

END

Eventually, I was placed on a bed like a boat
in an empty room with sky-filled windows,
with azure blue pillows, the leopard-like quilt.

It was English tea-time, with the kind of light
that electrifies the ordinary. It had just stopped raining.
Beads of water on glass glittered like secrets.

In another room they were baking, mulling wine.
I was warm with cloves, melting butter, demerara,
and wearing your pyjamas. My felt slippers

waited on the floor. Then the door opened
soundlessly, and I climbed out of bed.
It was like slipping on to the back of a horse,

and the room folded in, like a pop up story
then the house, and the Vale. Even the songs
and prayers tidied themselves into grooves

and the impossible hospital laid down its chimneys
its sluices, tired doctors, and waiting room chairs.
And I came here.   It was easy to leave.

APOLOGY FOR ABSENCE

Look, it's as if my heart is a damp cupboard
filled with old brass that needs polishing.

Or I must cover myself with moss, damp down,
try to establish new growth in the rotting.

Sometimes I am whipped to shreds by the North wind
and must curl up beneath a counterpane.

I need to practise dying, to imagine health,
to eat tinned pears, light unnecessary fires.

And love can by tyrannical, so sweet, yet edgy.
I am overpowered by its fragrant red roses.

Sitting rooms are too vivid. Things get torn.
I have to disappear, to darn each rip.

Forgive me, brave daughters, for the questions
that I have failed to answer. And my love,

please don't say I malingered, don't be
angry later, when you add up the ticks.

INDELIBLE, MIRACULOUS

friend, think of your breath
on a cold pane of glass

you can write your name there
with an outstretched finger

or frosted, untouched grass
in the early morning, a place

where you can dance alone
leave your footprints there

a deep pool of silver water
waits for you to make waves

the beach is clean after the storm
the tide has washed away yesterday

we all matter, we are all
indelible, miraculous, here

Julia Deakin

CODICIL

Hang about, Vicar, let me interrupt.
Having been full of life you say, I'd want a party.
Yes, but I'm full of death now and see things differently.
You say I wouldn't have wanted folk to grieve for long.
No – but with infinite death ahead of me,
a few months being alive and fed up
doesn't seem much to ask of my friends.

OK, some of you wear the bright clothes I admired –
but you lot with less taste, give us a break
and wear dark colours, please.
No flowers? Donations only? Hold your horses.
I could never have picked one charity
and loved buying and looking at flowers. I'd like to give
my mourners that opportunity.

True I liked food, and would like to see most of you
tucking in. But I'd also like to do some good –
and some of you who could do to lose a pound or two
should surely be too upset to eat.
Smile by all means, remember my gaffes
and share a careful laugh –

but then it's my funeral, fuck it –
some of you ought to go home and WEEP BUCKETS.

PRESCRIPTION

The wig sat at the bottom of the wardrobe
in a deep, square, dark blue box
like a hat or ashes or some strange stage prop.

They sent it out before you started chemo
so you wouldn't feel you couldn't face the world –
or if you stayed in wouldn't feel undressed, or cold.

You tried it, once. It sat on your thinned hair
like no hat anybody ever wore or hair they grew
but thicker, heavier, like dolls' hair – squeaky.

A shade too big (or standing off respectfully)
it shrank your scalp; your face and eyes, too quick,
seemed dislocated, swerving like caught prey.

It gave you, not the judge's gravitas you needed
or the panto dame's bravado, but the frailty
of someone carrying a dead weight.

Out there was comedy: Crown Toppers,
ferrets, Ernie Wise. We banished quips
until you made them – made us smile

as you, who'd never cared about appearance
but half each year had worn dad's socks around the house
took off the wig, turned it to the light

and felt the cavity inside:
the dull, flesh-coloured backing
where your warmth had been.

LOST

We call them lost, our loved ones, but if they are
just that – lost – wandering among the stars, faint
as our faith in heaven or hell, knowing other fates –

like that recurring dream of being lost in an echo
of a place where nothing's recognised and no one
recognises you, of wandering without a haven,
without welcome, without knowing where you are
except that you were, once, on earth but where is that,
oh mother, father, child, if you are more lost there
than you were here, what then? What then?

Barbara Dordi

WITH A BANG

This is not how it is supposed to be;
I had long imagined it would be quick,
sudden, over in a twink: no
goodbyes, no regrets, no last words.

This is not how it is supposed to be;
the knowing, yet not knowing when.
The waiting, though, gives me time to prepare
for what will now be a polished finish.

This is not how it is supposed to be;
the telephone never stops ringing:
dinners, exhibitions, trips to the Lakes,
the subject they dreaded, not taboo.

This is not how it is supposed to be;
I have put my own plans into action:

Schubert, a few straight words from a friend,
then jazz, so no black please, no flowers.

This is not how it is supposed to be;
for the first time, I feel I'm in control.
At the end, I know, I face it alone,
so let's party – to hell with the gravestone!

KNOWING

Did you know just how you drew me in –
Brushing my hair, chanting to me?
I knew
I always knew

Did you know my heartbeat was your rocking chair
Riding rough terrain of kitchen floor?
I knew
I always knew.

With steel poker you riddled the coals
Fire flaming the smouldering ashes.

Your grown-up tea in a china cup
Your buttered barnbrack straight from the oven.

Your pats and sighs and smiles cured all
Blackened kettle steaming assent.

Did you know as you lay, expecting to die
That I couldn't come to say goodbye?
I knew
I always knew.

Noreen Drake-Stoker

WHAT DO YOU THINK?

Each day I find myself
not getting used to being without you
but I discover new ways.

I spend a lot of time talking to you –
a one-sided conversation I know –
but then, we both know, I was used to that.

You never gave me the answer
though, somehow, I arrived at it
by going through the process

of answering your question –
sounds crazy, but that's how it used to be
and it still works.

Ann Drysdale

from *Scattering His Ashes*

DELIVERY FROM THE 'CREM'

The wooden box was passably presented;
It was the bag inside that made me cry.
The stapled see-through plastic I resented,
Although the box was passably presented –
You'd think the wit of man could have invented
Something more suited to a fond goodbye.
The box itself was passably presented.
It was the bag inside that made me cry.

FEEDING THE DUCKS AT CALSTOCK

This was one of the places we had shared.
I had imagined I would be alone;
The place was packed with grockles. I was scared
To make much ceremony on my own.
The smell of chips lay heavy on the air,
The day was hot, the Tamar brown and thick.
I needed to complete my business there
And felt it would be best if I were quick:
Off with the lid, a surreptitious fling.
A cloud of spinning bits sank in the murk
And, terrified of missing anything,
All the assembled wildfowl went berserk.
Feeding the ducks? I heard somebody say.
Something like that, I said, and turned away.

PLODGING AT WHITLEY BAY

The beach is deserted. I'll empty your tin
At the edge of the ocean. The tide's coming in
And the water will take you and make you a part
Of its practical purpose, its innocent art.
In the language of limestone it solemnly sings
Of corals and cliffs and ephemeral things.

Now the foam is encroaching as if it's aware of
The thing it's been given to love and take care of.
It curtseys and bobs with a coy little hiss
Then purses its lips in a whiskery kiss.
The flocculent fag-ash is eager to fly
But the little white hard bits refuse to comply.

So forward and back go the brisk little waters,
The sifters and winnowers, sharers and sorters
And when it is over the thing is decided,
You are played-for and won; you are lost and divided.

You are part of the ocean and part of the land
Dispersed in the sea and ensconced in the sand.

from *Coming to Terms*

GOODNIGHT HARRY *(Tuesday 11th September 2012)*

A sudden need to ring and speak to you,
to say *Hello, my love – I'm on the train*,
became a desolation, and I knew
that you and I will never meet again.
I'm going home and we have said goodbye.
I will be back, just as I said I would,
but others with a greater right than I
need time for their farewells. Ours was for good.
We have exchanged our promises at last
and uttered most of what we meant to say.
You know that I'll preserve our precious past;
I understand that there is *but one way* –
your raised hand, your surprised eyes following,
a way of saying that green fields were beckoning.

FRESH AIR *(Sunday 23rd September 2012)*

I woke up on my own side of the bed
and scrabbled for my slippers on the floor,
slowly remembering that you were dead
and there was nothing left to hurry for.
Your own remains had been attended to
and all our correspondence burned and scattered.
In a few hours we'd be cremating you,
making an end to everything that mattered.
I pushed the window open, just a tad,
guiltily thinking how you had been certain
that cold air was 'a draught' and therefore bad.
I felt it on my face and drew the curtain
to let what you were so suspicious of
blow gently over all that unmade love.

ANYONE FOR TENNIS?

I miss the frisson of our special match,
the old reliable relationship;
sure of a hand to hold, an eye to catch,
the merry to-and-fro of quirk and quip.
Sometimes we'd lob a thought across the net,
languidly vamping till one saw a shot
and made a volley to secure the set
with a divine one-liner. Now I've got
no wit-reflector, no beloved grin.
I try to rally but, without the same
perfect collusion you and I were in,
I'm by myself, playing a different game.
I serve in hope, only to see the ball
drop at the foot of an enormous wall.

WINTER CAMPING

One thing was always understood between us.
When you were ready to go Winter Camping
I would not be a part of the adventure.

You bought equipment and wrote plans in journals,
Calling it Personal Development,
Anticipating solitude and challenge.

You never did it. Life got in the way
Until death stopped the prospect altogether.
I have not often thought about it since.

Sleeping without you was a big adventure.
A single bed, electrically warmed,
Beside the open door on to the balcony.

Birds visited. Various gastropods
Slid over the threshold and were welcome.
Cats came and went. Last night there was a storm.

I went to sleep enchanted by the wind.
It died in the small hours; the silence woke me.
I am in an extraordinary place.

Dark, starred with tiny lights across the valley,
Clouded with frozen breath. I move carefully,
Explore the limits of my warm cocoon.

Now on my left there is a precipice.
Cold fingers trace the edges of my ears.
I am alone and this is Winter Camping.

Carol Ann Duffy

COLD

It felt so cold, the snowball which wept in my hands,
yet when I rolled it along in the snow, it grew
till I could sit on it, looking back at the house,
where it was cold when I woke in my room, the windows
blind with ice, my breath undressing itself on the air.
Cold, too, embracing the torso of snow which I lifted up
in my arms to build a snowman, my toes, burning, cold
in my winter boots; my mother's voice calling me in
from the cold. And her hands were cold from peeling
then dipping potatoes into a bowl, stopping to cup
her daughter's face, a kiss for both cold cheeks, my cold nose.
But nothing so cold as the February night I opened the door
in the Chapel of Rest where my mother lay, neither young, nor old,
where my lips, returning her kiss to her brow, knew the meaning of cold.

Jane Duran

HAIRPINS

The downpour comes to our house.
All our rooms are ablaze with that inevitable
inconsolable darkness before it ceases

in every room of the house, every part of the woods,
the screened-in porch and white-wood corridor
leading to the window and the whippoorwill

that will turn itself to dust with its song
night after night, cooped up in the willow;
fences and barns and ponds that recede in the rain

but are really constants in my life, come in close,
the pewter magnifying glass on the dresser
magnifying each hour.

My grandmother piles her hair loosely with hairpins.
The hairpins won't hold, never, in that heavy grey.
I push them back for her, her forgetfulness,

and the long summer is almost over
in those few lazy drops that still
drip from the trees and eaves in a lasting vigil.

CAPE PORPOISE, MAINE

I go back to that walk,
island to island
across the mind at low tide —

the sun that dips down
or the flaring sun, dismissing the houses
on the cape, that dimension of the jutting houses

and the way the wind shows them
and then deepens suddenly and is all around me
like a person I know well

and the occasional broken shells
like my mother's unfinished sentences,
her childhood memories I still enjoy visiting.

I go back so I can walk
past my own past into hers
though the tide will come in soon –

as no solution, and with no ambition
but to roll up my bluejeans
and walk where the water was.

Sarianne Durie

TRAVELLING ALONE

Through country lanes to reach the Inn
brown and black cows crest the hill –
dark green thicket on the left – a single
tree to the right. Loneliness
is drawn in a thin line of brown and black
across the hill and stands waiting by the tree.

A single menu at table, quiet evening walk
swallows and martins make their massed rush
into egg-green seashell skies –

single cuckoos already gone and swifts
have fled the changing weather.

Families stand and stare at transplanted vegetation
flowering, foreign, in Eden's new rainforest
under domed glass sky – linger here
hurry there – you do not belong – out of place
out of couple – you have become
invisible – draw the thin line after you.
Your footsteps leave no trace
your shadow already gone.

WHAT JUDITH SAYS

I talk to dead friends all the time
and they talk to me –
sometimes I have them call me on the phone
it's very comforting

I like to hear their voices
though we don't have long conversations –
it's more a matter of sound and tone –
I often take my grandmother to concerts
it gives her pleasure that I'm there

This seems perfectly reasonable to me –
though many friends would think
me indulgent or
not prepared
to accept reality or
maybe even – nuts
I am not really of the stiff-upper-lip school
I know people should get on with it –
but I also think they should mourn
keen and carry on however they like

Neil Elder

GRIEF–STRICKEN

What strikes me is the way grief
clings to you like wet clothes.
What pains me is that you have grown
into them as though they are a second skin.

I remember returning from school,
soaked through and dripping.
Get those clothes off quick –
They'll be the death of you.

Roger Elkin

MARKING TIME
(for Eileen Boon)

There's his diving-watch:
somehow chubby, snub-nosed, squat:
his blunt reminder of time:

its face the black of his sub-aqua suit;
its one-eyed lens, sibling of the goggle-mask
that made his face Cyclops, almost alien;

and its satin-finished wrist-band
with that clasp he snapped secure
like his cupping embrace.

So there's nothing to distract
about it: masculine, no-nonsense,
deadly practical, necessary

like the oxygen lungs
they strapped to his back
that took him down, then up again.

Could withstand pressure – lots.
Was proof against water, and salt:
but knew the witness of tears.

So remains, marking time:
its silent movement
husbanding these empty hours.

BOXING SAFELY AWAY MY FOSTER-MOTHER'S ROSARY

I've lived with it till leaving her,
that string of seed-pod beads –
fragile, antique, shiny-bright as tears –
wired to skin-thin discs depicting
Our Lady resplendent in silvery grace,
embossed with *Souvenir de Lourdes,*
and, beneath, a miniature crucifix
with Christ distended in suffering –
so much torn agony, such pain
for ordinary folk to carry around.

What miles of guilt and forgiveness
I've witnessed her pale hands journeying
in those daily Hail Marys and
ritual silences she put between us
with index finger-lifts of shushing.
So, it comes as no surprise that she's
picked me to receive the single thing
she thought fit for passing down, to keep it
safe, slithering through my riddling fingerings.

She'll never know that after the wake
once we've put our lives back together,
I'll box up that chain of faith, then slide it
deep inside the console drawer.

That way, hiding away her parades
of silences from my kids' enquiring hands,
I'll create for us a grace of sorts
that knows no display of pain,
no show of guilt, no hurt of minds,
just love, no strings attached.

June English

RIVERSFLOW
(a haven on the River Dour)

The undertaker wants Dad's shoes. The thought
of him just lying there, his pin-stripe suit –
and best white shirt, his work-worn naked feet –
probably shouting, *Where's my bloody boots!*

He always called shoes *boots*. I polish them
and stow them in my bag. *It's time to go;*
how strange it seems, knowing I won't see him,
won't hear his *Giddy up to Riversflow*....
My hands shake as I close the door. *Don't cry,*
I tell myself. *You've got a task to do.*
Dad's face appears, pastiched on passers-by;
I know he's dead, but can't believe it's true.

The streets seem changed, until I pass the Co-op.
Stop. Go back, gather courage, look inside,

believing, in that moment, that he'll pop
his head out, call, *I'll see you later, mind*

you tell thee Mum I've bought scrag-end of lamb.
But he's not there. I hug his shoes and stride
with more determined steps. It won't take long –
five hundred yards, turn left, bear right, then straight....

I'm ushered in, spoken to in low, slow tones,
asked: *Would you like to see your father now?*
His waxen face and hollow cheeks, stark bones,
owe nothing to the Dad I love and know –

he's all of that and more at Riversflow:
the sun's his warm embrace, the rustling leaves
his *Well done, thank you, love.* The kiss he blows
a fragrant *See, I told thee not to grieve....*

GATHERING LILAC

She was always going somewhere....

Those last five years she died with me
were spent in gathering lilac.
I don't know who you are my dear,
but thanks a lot, how kind you've been.
I hope we'll meet again quite soon.
Then I'd be Mum and hold her tight,
and beg her stay a little while,
remind her how we used to sing
We'll Gather Lilac in the Spring.

She was always going somewhere....

Those last five years she died with me
were spent in gathering lilac.
A policeman brought her back one day,
a naked mouse in an overcoat;
she spat and screamed and scratched at me
as if I'd sprung the trap that nailed her.
I took her by the hand and sang
the words she knew and loved so well,
she held me close, my Mum until –

she was always going somewhere....

Those last five years she died with me
were spent in gathering lilac.
She'd pack her handbag furtively:
a comb, a photograph of Dad,
a twig cut from the lilac tree.
Put out the light! The Warden's here!
Your father's legs are weeping shrapnel.

She was always going somewhere....

Those last few years she died with me.
I don't know who you are my dear
But thanks a lot. How kind you've been.
I said *Goodnight, God bless you Mum*
We'll Gather Lilac in the Spring.

Carrie Etter

A BIRTHMOTHER'S CATECHISM

(September 11, 1986)

How did you let him go?
With black ink and legalese
How did you let him go?
It'd be another year before I could vote
How did you let him go?
With altruism, tears, and self-loathing
How did you let him go?
A nurse brought pills for drying up breast-milk
How did you let him go?
Who hangs a birdhouse from a sapling?

A BIRTHMOTHER'S CATECHISM

What is the anniversary of loss?
A national day of mourning
Really now, what is the anniversary of loss?
My mother and I watch TV well past her usual bedtime
What is the anniversary of loss?
Where the swan's nest had been, widely scattered branches and some
crumpled beer cans
What is the anniversary of loss?
Sometimes the melancholy arrives before the remembering
What is the anniversary of loss?
Some believe it is impossible to spend too much on the memorial
What is the anniversary of loss?
When I say sometimes the melancholy comes first, I know the body has
its own memory
What is the anniversary of loss?
The wishbone snapped, and I clung to the smaller piece

A BIRTHMOTHER'S CATECHISM

Who do you think you are?
A musical phrase remembered from time to time for no apparent reason
Who do you think you are?
A wrong answer
Who do you think you are?
An aptitude for words his parents do not share
Who do you think you are?
The vestige of an unacknowledged longing
Who do you think you are?
Eve
Who do you think you are?
No one, no one at all

U A Fanthorpe

SONG

Don't eavesdrop on my heart,
  It's a sneak.
It will chat with any stranger,
Lifeguard, lover, doctor, tailor;
It just needs to feel an ear
  And it will speak.

Don't eavesdrop on my heart,
  It's illiterate.
The educated hand, eye, brain,
Turn words to shapes and back again;
My stupid heart could never learn
  The alphabet.

Don't eavesdrop on my heart,
  It's dumb.

In rainforests of tubes and pumps
It hangs, my heart, a third-world dunce;
Parrots can speak, but my heart just
   Communicates by drum.

Don't eavesdrop on my heart,
   It's clever.
And if your head should touch my breast
My heart would make its own arrest
Develop hands, as trees grow leaves,
   And hold you there forever.

IDYLL

Not knowing even that we're on the way,
Until suddenly we're there. How shall we know?

There will be blackbirds, in a late March evening,
Blur of woodsmoke, whisky in grand glasses,

A poem of yours, waiting to be read; and one of mine;
A reflective bitch, a cat materialised

On a knee. All fears of present and future
Will be over, all guilts forgiven.

Maybe, heaven. Or maybe
We can get so far in this world. I'll believe we can.

BREAK

(Charing Cross Road to Wotton-under-Edge)

A mistake, perhaps, to have mentioned *The Waste Land?*
The heat-wave cracked while we were at the reading

In a London cellar. Sweltering, parched, we surfaced
Into vicious urban rain. The car, three brollies in it,
Was £3.50 away; we skulked by *The Mousetrap;*
I fussed about phoning; the A–Z got soaked
(Its print too small anyway) round Lisson Grove.
How had we got there? I wanted an ice,
You bought me nougat. We were on
The verge of a quarrel.

Then suddenly the two of us burst out singing.
Not the usual, *Jerusalem, Down Ampney, Cwm Rhondda*
But foreign territory, *Danny Boy,*
The Ash Grove and *Loch Lomond.*
You held the tenor, as you always do,
I clung to the treble with my raucous squeak,
Not hearing you in case I lost the tune,

Then found myself descanting, bang in the middle
Of *The Foggy Foggy Dew,* kept it up through *The Ploughboy.*
So we did it all over again, three times three.
I reached notes nature didn't intend me for,
And heard both you and me, and wasn't thrown.
Suddenly, in the wet and the dark, we burst out singing,
And I said *Is jazz like this?* and you said *It is.*

Our voices gave out at Bibury. I don't expect
A second coming, or need one. Enough
Once in a lifetime to be part of the song.

WINTERSPORTS

Winter is rook. He blunders stiffly
Down four hard months, darkness being
His mute barrage. Sometimes he over-reaches
Into power-cuts, snow, fog. Then humanity,

Staging survival, the child's romp, swapping
Paraffin, antifreeze, anecdotes, becomes
Humane. Endless gentle erosion,
If only he knew, is his most mortal finesse.

The wretched are king; powerless,
And so beautiful. We revere them,
Comfort them with drugs, parlour games,
Short walks on sunny days, and are
At last checked by their endless
Vulnerability.

I endure winter, and the punctual
Attendance of the distressed
With the pawn's continuous midget acts
Of gallantry. But your absence is
Knight's move, the jagged cut
Clean across expectation.
I have no defence against it.

CHAPLAINCY FELL WALK

There is always one out in front
With superior calves and experienced boots;

Always a final pair to be waited for,
Not saying much, pale, rather fat;

And the holy ones in the middle, making it
Their part to acclimatise the lonely and new,
Introducing cinquefoil, a heron, a view;

And a stout one who giggles, uniting us
In wonder at her unfaltering chokes;
But alarming too. For what is she laughing at?

And remote presence of hills;
And the absence of you.

QUEUEING OUTSIDE THE *JEU DE PAUME* IN LIGHT RAIN

If you were here
I'd ask the smiling African
In my slow-motion French what makes his birds
Rattle their paper wings, and fly, and fall
Beside his hand. *Gilly-gilly-gilly,* he woos us all,
Very good, very nice. For you he'd laugh,
And tell.

If you were here
Something profound about his airy art,
The art we queue for under our umbrellas,
Would bounce between us, jokily. You'd note

The grace of our neighbours' passing-the-time conversation
(Mind you, Muriel says it's always raining in Paris.
And she lives here).

I have grown expert on your absences. I know
How things would differ, how the resolute
Mock-bird would tangle frailly with my feet,
And how you'd buy it, just because it did,
And you were there.

ELEGY FOR A CAT

Yours was the needlework, precise and painful
As claws on a loved naked shoulder, that sewed us
Back into that Merthyr morning, when, terrorised by toddlers,
You mined under our alien gateway, claimed sanctuary
In a jacket pocket.

You were the first to join our outlandish outfit
On that hilltop housing estate, with the garage-in-name-only,
Invisible agog neighbours, rhubarb corms from Aberfan;
You the first source of our logged jokes, with
Your ears akimbo,

Eyes so excited they retreated behind their withers,
Living a paw-to-mouth existence, elbowing your way
Up bodies like a midshipman up rigging
Your whiskers wet with passion, sitting with one ear
In a human mouth, to keep warm.

I was never sure that English was your language,
Though you were probably just as dim in Welsh,
Vague about status, doglike coming to a whistle,
Running on white bandy-legs with a
Welcoming cluck.

You never took offence, were always ready
With an Eskimo kiss of your pink plebeian nose;
Set records for slow learning when we installed
The cat-flap; had no idea of the gravitas
Proper to cats.

Exiled in Gloucestershire, you domesticated
It for us, materialised on preoccupied laps, and,
Mozart-addict, rushed in filthy-footed from
Uprooting lupins, to settle yourself round Primo's collar
When duets began.

Now the heir's installed, she colonises
The outposts (both next-doors, and one further)
Where she's feasted and fêted. Such cunning
Is natural to your prudent race, in case
Of catastrophe.

And I see, dear dead one, how we severed you
From your own earth, how you chose us to be
Your territory. You are there quite often,
Dear tabby blur, in my bad eye's corner. We left you
Nothing to haunt but ourselves.

Haunt us still, dear first-footer,
First to live with us, first to confirm
Us as livers-together, you who took us so simply
For granted, translator of life into
The vernacular of love.
You who saw love, where innocent others
Saw only convenience.

TOMORROW AND

(i.m. J.R. who read Cowper while dying of cancer)

Was and *will be* are both uneasy ground;
Now is the safest tense.

Terminal Care rests among recipes
On the kitchen table.

We choke the future back down our throats like
Incipient vomit,

With so much time ahead, for all we know,
For turning out cupboards,

Pottery courses, Greek holidays, Brahms,
Grandchildren, greenhouses,

Getting at last to the end of
Decline and Fall of the Roman

It's all indifferent to him. He won't
Be here. Our small concerns

Balk us with their familiarity.
His perspectives are strict.

Library fines and income tax returns
Have lost their sting. The huge

Ghouls that shadow old age have excused him.
His exacting lover

Arrogates all of him. He'll never grow
Senile, tiresome, lonely.

With stoic courtesy, unfortified
By rites of holy church,

He watches each tomorrow, appraises
Contour, climate, colour,

As if it were a new world, while his books
(Which he won't read again,

He says) rest idle on their shelves, and nights
Grow longer, and contain

More symptoms, and his friends come, go, come, go,
Swallowing hereafters,

And he transacts the same
Miniature feats of gallantry with which
Cowper restrained the dark

Once, as far as we know

THE PASSING OF ALFRED

*He [Tennyson] died with his hand on his Shakespeare, and the moon shining full into the window over him . . . A worthy end. (*Queen Victoria: *Journal)*

Our fathers were good at dying.
They did it lingeringly,
As if they liked it; correctly,
With earnest attention to detail,
Codicils brought up to date,
Forgiveness, confession, last-gasp
Penitence properly witnessed
By responsible persons. Attorneys,
Clerics, physicians, all knew their place
In the civil *pavane* of dying.

Households discharged
Their methodical duties: said farewell
In order of precedence, outdoor staff first,
Faithful hounds respectfully mourning,
Lastly the widow-to-be, already
Pondering a transformed wardrobe.

They died in the houses,
The beds they were born in,
They died where they lived, between
Known sheets, to the obbligato
Of familiar creaks and ticks.

We who differ, whose dears are absorbed
Into breezy wards for routine terminations,
Envy our fathers their decorous endings
In error. Nothing makes extinction easy.
They also died appallingly, over
The family breakfast-cups; bloodily
In childbed; graveyard coughed themselves
Into coffins; declined from heart-break
And hunger. And however resigned,

Orderly, chaste, aesthetic the passing of Alfred,
Remorse, regret still shadowed the living after.

Like us they ran from habit to tell good news
To dead ears; like us they dreamed
Of childhood, and being forgiven;
And the dead followed them, as they do us,
Tenderly through darkness,
But fade when we turn to look in the upper air.

THE DYING MAN AND THE LOVERS

He knows he hasn't long. His hungry eye
Eats all it sees, but slowly, for the taste
And smell of living must be relished first.

They know they've all their lives to satisfy
A mutual appetite, but time is waste
While they're apart. Saying good night is worst.

He wants each moment lengthened into years.
A woodlouse is a miracle of life.
No one's a chance acquaintance; all are friends.

Cocooned in webs of love, their eyes and ears
Are dead to us. Honeymoon, husband, wife,
Are new learned words with unimagined ends.

His happiness ignores himself. He sees
How tender and how fragile all things are.
Dying makes him opaque; the world grows clear.

Bewitched, obsessed, they assume sympathies.
The world contracts to fit their formula.
Horizons shred along his last frontier.

Geraldine Farrow

FOLDS

When I unsquash the pads of my thumb and forefinger
they stay flat for minutes.
When I bend my wrist forward skin folds
in ripples like a tired tide without a moon.
My skin used to be plump and springy –
now, it wrinkles and tears like tissue paper.

If I could lay my aging skin neatly
fold upon fold, maybe I could enfold time.
I would go back to a late spring evening
in the garden, you and I sipping tea
on a blue painted seat. When you say,
Of course I'll be all right on my own.
I stay with you anyway.

Beverley Ferguson

OUTPATIENTS APPOINTMENT

In our meeting a mobile phone rings
my doctor answers it and says:
I am with a female at the moment.
I look down. I see my strong lifeline
running as a long thread curving
across the cobweb of my open palm.
The full moon white like soft foam
leaves a shadowed imprint on my skin
marking me for madness. I look up.
In that moment I have become female,
late fifties. Married with one son.

Two hospital admissions, very long.
I breathe out gently frosting the room.
I have become a female so he carries on.

ILLNESS

I do not recognise myself in the mirror
I see loneliness which has followed me
from hospital and found me in my room.

When I came home you had painted
these walls, choosing the colour pink
from flowers woven into my Persian rug,

bringing in something of the outside. Windows
on the ward were not allowed to be fully opened.
I have become used to not being seen.

Victoria Field

FORGET-ME-NOTS

A constellation of blue eyes
    that cannot look this way

Insistent names, calling out
    with nothing at all to say

A frilled and speckled counterpane
    with no small soul asleep

A dancing, posing prettiness
    but no lock of hair to keep

A scattering of loveliness
    that won't take shape nor grow

I'll remember you who never were
    and can neither come nor go.

Anthony Fisher

I WOULD CRY

What would I want to have?
Your smile, the one only I see.
I would catch it in a mirror
hang it in my heart.

I'd keep your shoes in the hall,
left toe turned in,
the way you step out of them,
pretend that you'd just arrived.

What could I leave you
to be there whenever you want?
Not my breath on your neck
to be soon washed away.

It would be our memories,
laughter and skin's embrace,
secret messages,
and that's what I would want to have.

Rose Flint

HORSES IN THE SUMMERLANDS

Horses like snow volcanoes, ruled by love.
Horses like bronze bells, rung by love.
Coloured horses, thick-ankled,
mapping a possible landscape, a continent
called faraway-from-here. Horses like dun birds,
like red burs, like fire-dragons whooshing up
and over fences, my thought, my heart.
Horses with long wide warm white necks
curved round so their nostrils were close, their breath
(grass-sweet) beside my hair and my hot eyes;
their sweat's sweetness, the horse-sweetness
of hay and dung and the long fields of the summerlands.
Horses who leaped and leaped over the high boundaries
that held all the hurts together in one sharp mass,
leaped like legends with wings and I went with them, leaping
and racing and sliding in the marsh-field at the forest edge
and just for a moment I had slipped out of the grip
of the dead mother and maths and my father's eyes –
because I couldn't do maths even if I could fly
and just for a moment receive the blessing
of breath so laden with sweetness it was
as if a hand stroked my hair.

Kate Foley

MY FATHER, COUNTING SHEEP

He has been awake
for long enough, counting.
His life is thick, painful
seconds, squeezed from the glass.
Stretching his eyes behind
the sharp sun's lance
he waits
for the terrible medicine of dark.

He has his mother's eyes.
Often she rapped his head
with bony knuckles,
her fierce hazel glint
searching out sin like truffles.

She never cured him of looking;
silk in the rag bag,
silver in the clouds.

Now, his rib cage winnowed
with scorching breath,
his big glove puppet hands
tell their own story
to the sheets.

Somewhere in the dry
fields of his brain
he is driving his last
ragged thoughts relentlessly,

over and over,
past the same gate,
counting to keep awake.

What gives him quiet?
Not me with my bolus
of love and drugs.
My mother, her voice

shrill with familiar strain,
whispers angrily tender:
let GO! He sighs.
His flocks line up soberly.
All the mild sheep
are folded through his eyes.

THROWN

I bought death for our cat;
the needle, drug and vet
to kill her pain.

As I buried her, an ant
walked over one green
translucent eye.

It is relief to turn
to larger deaths. Megaliths,
part of a growing circle,

they stand so tall,
so other, so far beyond
effect of mine, that pain

is like the ant
on my cat's dead eye –
irrelevant.

I butt my head against
their granite sides;
I cannot move them.

Great stone cattle, they give
no milk, or blood; as cold
and far from tears as clouds.

It is cats and birds and empty
slippers; small lives lost
that move the stone;

they are the pebble
on which your heel turns
to bring death home.

Angela France

TELL THE BEES

Something has plundered the bees' nest
at the wall's foot where lichened brick
used to meld into a tangle of moss and ivy:
a ragged tear now bleeds earth over the path.
Bees tread circles on the spilled soil,
wings quivering, shifting grains from place
to place and back again.

Each day I pass, I see them working;
fragments of moss, scatters of dried grass,
pulled in to cover their loss.
They can't fill the space.

The sun has faded bare earth,
shrivelled exposed roots.
Ivy leans over the edge of the hole,
blending into the dusty green
of the bees' repairs.

AFTER THE PHONE CALL

            air thickened,
radio voices vibrated and slowed
to a memory of deep water.
Words, phrases, bubbled up
from the call; jangled, garbled,
making no sense.

Thoughts scurry like rats in a drain;
of flights and affording them,
of time off work,
of cancelling appointments,
of costs and overdrafts,
as if there was time.
            as if there were still time.

COUNTING THE CUNNING WAYS

Corpse-hounds, he calls them, or lych-birds,
turns away from their churring call. He curses
a white moth in the house, slaps at its blunder
against a dusty bulb. He'll take a long way round
to avoid meeting a hearse head-on, shudder
to see a child point at the plumed horses.
He won't take the ashes out after sundown,
always comes and goes by the same door,
shouts at ravens to chase them from the roof.
He won't wear anything new to a funeral
and covers his head by an open grave.
The bird in the house, the left eye's twitch,
hawthorn indoors, a mirror cracked.
So many ways to foretell death and disaster;
but it came for him while he wasn't looking.

Wendy French

IN LIMBO
(i.m.J.F.)

So different from Guy's, no outdated anti-smoking sign, just
the usual well-thumbed magazines and leaflets
offering massage, homeopathy. The nurse adjusts
the giddy tubes, checks the intravenous drip,
changes pads, so we, the visitors to this other world
can leave assured, it's safe, secure to house the dying.

Death here is softly sprung, neutral coloured,
no squeaking up corridors, no clanking trolleys.
The notes from Bach's cello concerto come from somewhere
I can't see; this digging down to find what lies beneath.
We're here counting each movement as an open
wound waits for healing. The nurse will come, say the unsayable
but all I can think of is you, so adaptable
and how you said you'll learn to love the dark.

CITY ROAD

Me, walking down City Road, Islington,
me on a hot, hot day scorching the earth

with plodding feet,
intent on tying these sunflowers – wilting –

to railings and my mum following, sighing.
Deep sighs roar against the traffic,

and me, frustrated by the horns and dust
and men in pinstripes rushing as if they are

the only ones on a mission. I'm glad to be walking
except I had to retrace my steps as the florist

I'd intended to go to – the one near the railings –
was closed on Wednesdays and I had to walk

back to the Angel, the flowers less fresh,
more expensive, now in my arms.

Thinking about the canal and the houseboat,
empty. Yesterday it was hers, now it belongs to no one:

at twenty six you don't make a will. And then I notice
an abandoned bicycle chained to a post, two wheels gone,

whether the owner took them as an added precaution
or whether an opportunist had stolen them, who knows?

Me worrying about something futile on today of all days.
The bicycle's forgotten as the sound of a busker

from outside St Mary's is playing, Ellington, *A Train*
in a London street where God is nowhere

and me, stopped midway to listen and my mum's voice,
How can the sky be so blue on a day like this?

THREE YEARS ON

no longer will I come to you (Sappho fragment 114)

This morning's early light woke my thoughts, July eight.
It would have been your thirtieth year.
I go to Iceland for the midnight sun.

Campers under sun-capped mountains.
Tiny churches silhouetted on the edge – houses, sheep,
horses descended from Viking days. A country of lupins, buttercups.

When I was young I believed the dead were driven in taxis to the stars.
No taxi to take us to heaven on dirt roads which circled round
the impenetrable centre of cracked earth.

In Iceland God was hiding in a shepherd's croft.
Every evening morning disappears
and all the fields you ever ran around

are soaked in twilight.
This present seems motionless.
Everything, slow. *Bullshit,* you say, *move on.*

The earth's crust is thin. Huge craters to fall through.
Continental plates separating
and in the distance two fishermen slide out of focus.

Warnings about pot-holes in the road.
All disappear against the light. And Iceland cut in two
by the Mid-Atlantic ridge – drifting away from herself.

Each morning you're newly gone.

Leah Fritz

ENDGAME

It's been a party. That I know
            now that it's nearly over.
We promised we'd leave together.
            Fall out of a plane
                    holding hands. Jump
        from one of the towers.
                No chance.

You had your bit of surgery,
I've something in my blood.
                We'll go our
separate ways, one before.
        The other
                        at last.

Cynthia Fuller

REVENANT

In dreams you mingle
with the living, inhabiting
your old live self, convincing –
almost – that not a single
moment should be lost in grieving.

Asleep, a part of me is hopeful –
how much I want to believe,
to breathe in deep relief;
a part is wary, mistrustful,
remembering that well of grief.

Waking, I turn in time – almost –
to see you cross back over.
You leave behind a tremor
in the air, shadows and dust,
empty space becoming emptier.

CHANGES

Her change to widow
changed me into friend.
I held her grief like heavy wool
for her to wind,
ached with importance,
a stiff friend
who dreamed her skirts grew wide enough
to hide in.
My love was nourished by safe walls.
Cut loose
I feared to fail her.

NO FAIRY STORY
(for D.H.J. 1907-1975)

She didn't need a magic mirror.
Her presence was so strong in me
that even when she wasn't there
I knew she might be. Too honest to lie to,
she was a stream too clear to muddy.

The one time that I really needed her
she came like Demeter across the miles,
straight from the top step of the ladder
not waiting to brush the distemper
from her hair. She came with her belief,
lighting small tapers in the deepest dark.

Now she would be a hundred – thinking
conjures her back across the gulf.
She's covering the years in seven league
strides, scattering all the stars in her wake.

TIME TRAVEL

My mother comes to visit from the dead.
Her dead clothes are a black cloche hat, a dusty coat,
all fire and colour drained and tired, the journey was
a long one. I nurse her, give her the grandsons
she should have known. She gathers strength enough
to explore with me a city full of flights of stairs,
grey narrow mazes where we search for something.
And then I lose her. Up steep steps I run wild and sobbing
for the small dusty woman who has come so far.
You were on the wrong stairs, she says, smiling.
In the street the sun is shining, buildings are golden.
A clock chimes the quarter. *My train back leaves*
at ten to. That I could let her miss it wakes me
back in the stretching desert of my loss.

Ray Fussell

BETTY BIRD

In the Star, he was the same,
three or four pints, talk of barmy
army trips, football, totty, salacious
gossip of 'C' list celebs.

At work he was the same,
designing parts of jigs and tools,

lunch break with a fag, then back on the drawing board,
his journey to work, last night on the telly.

At home, it was almost the same.
He could cook, load the dishwasher,
make his sandwiches just as he liked them.
Pete's wife came round to iron his shirts.

When he went to her purse, it was different.
He had no right to the small change of her life,
the notes folded her way, the plastic cards
bearing her name or the little brass safety pin.

Rory Gale

WHERE'S THE BABY?

Bright white lights
And white-washed walls,
Gloom is ever-present in the waiting-room.

At his bedside we find
His head lolls uselessly,
Eyes unfocused and innocent.

Where's the baby? he asks.

A shunt, they say, will redirect the fluid.

Where's the baby then?

Babble. Gleam of sweat
Present on his nurse-shaved cheeks,
The hole they've drilled into his skull

Drives closer to my heart.
Light falling on it shines
Like the great abyss his life has become.

But where's the baby?

Born 15 years ago,
I'm too tearful to talk,

This time he's gone too far.

Katherine Gallagher

CLOUD-EYE
(i.m. C.G.)

The sting in a limbering spring day
foreshadows summer. Through her window
roses plait themselves together beside young-
leafed eucalypts as she, too ill to speak,
slowly becomes my eye in the clouds, the gap
I will see through. No one knows me better
than she who circled my first flight.

I've tried to prepare myself, remembering
her cyclopaedic mind, her gift for solutions.
My bird-mother. I reach out, hold her hands.
She slides down into sleep and wakes again
on this final island, where touch is more important
than words. She grimaces, begs for morphine....
Our world divides. We'll fly differently now.

THE LONG REACH OUT OF WAR

They will keep restoring the glass
in broken cathedrals

to carry the eye and the colours
that were shattered

They will keep restoring the stone
in bombed cathedrals

to carry the face and the idea
that were crushed

They will keep carrying the burden
of destroyed cathedrals

even as the ashes blow back

Humanity
keeping faith with itself
even as the ashes blow back

Frances Galleymore

THE LOST CHILDREN

are all of us.
His photo tugged you on to the ocean:
the ferry carries you to your father.
The boat is big and its heart
is hidden with no beat
but a tremble in the rail beneath your hands.
Look how the sea is feathered and parted.
It heals without a scar

becoming whole again
while the old land is growing small.
On the deck beside you stands the child I was,
held fast, watching.
Your eyes are turned toward the seed and source
winging a water arrow
through gathered-in time.

Chrissie Gittins

REGISTRAR

She writes in pale blue indelible
across the ruled page –

place of birth, cause of death.
In time, the ink will darken to slate.

Later still, the veins of her letters
will fill with indigo.

My father's blood drained from his face
to gather at his spine.

His chilly skin, still smooth and soft,
was what I recognised.

She writes with care, her vowels round,
Ischaemic Heart Disease.

Through her blouse
are flicks of lace.

Her pumping heart is near.

THERE ARE THINGS I MUST REALISE YOU CAN NO LONGER DO

There are things I must realise you can no longer do –
climb the hill that was the view from your window
where we've climbed and talked of the past,
eat with a familiar wooden-handled spoon,
sleep in that narrow bed pushed hard against the wall.

Now this corridor contains your wandering,
or you are wedged into a chair with a hospital trolley.
There are no doors in your mind to say
this is a true story, that is not.
A nurse can talk about your inconsistency
whilst wearing perfect make-up.
A doctor wants to know if you can pay for your care.

From the mercury rush of your words
there are still some stones to gather –
You'll have a good drink of coffee before you go?
Make a sandwich – you can get them pre-wrapped now.
I always wanted to protect you.

The veins in your hands stretch like a washing line
pegged with the sheet of your skin.
The man in the opposite bed is wearing your watch.

Geoffrey Godbert

REMEMBERING

I remember my mother
and her aching love of film-stars.

I remember my brother
throwing darts against my skin.

I remember the silence
when my father was ridiculed.

I remember being told
my mother had lost a baby girl.

I remember a posh aunt
who managed a laundry.

I remember an old photograph
of the car that broke my father's wrist.

I remember him proudly drinking
Mateus Rosé when he'd made it.

I remember wishing the world
would swallow me up

when he played a piano
in a city music shop.

Then I remember escaping
by learning new words by heart

and singing them as if larks
were ascending like poetry.

Most of all, I remember
a James Joyce book I loaned

to a friendly bookshop each Monday
and on pay-day bought it back.

AT SUCH TIMES
(i.m. J L Carr)

For some of us
                    there will always
be the beating of a heart
to mark the precious moment
which has gone.
                    We can only ask
hopelessly for the return
of what once seemed ours for ever:
the way things looked
a voice remembered
the touch of a hand
a face we loved.

But now that they have gone
we just have to wait
                    hoping
our memories will never
pass and life will always
come back
            especially
and even
            at such times as this.

Dawn Gorman

A QUICK CURVE

They have not closed the road
from Marrakech airport,
so the traffic makes
a quick curve around
the crunched bicycle,
and the boy.
He is on his side,
a recovery position
from which he will not
rise, a white chalk line
around his head
shoulders
body
legs
feet.
It pins him as surely as a butterfly
in a case
to his final moment.
Those light blue jeans he bought,
so pleased at the good deal,
pulled on in haste this morning,
no thought that he would never
take them off.
His mother,
still in the market,
buys mutton for his supper,
not feeling
yet
the sudden smack
of the red and black wall
that waits to stop
her every thought
stone dead.

Rebecca Goss

KEEPING HOUSTON TIME

When they were told their son had died,
in a car, in America, he went into the greenhouse
and dismembered a dead bird.
He laid pieces out on a spade,
with splinters of beak around its head
like some gruesome halo.
When she came to the doorway
he looked up from his homemade angel
and with a candour that rarely came easily,
said he'd never loved his boy enough.
She looked at her watch, keeping Houston time,
and worked out he'd died while she was sleeping.
He died while we were sleeping, Jack,
were the only words she could say to him.

STOPPING DISTANCE

She threw her wedding ring into the long grass
of their garden two years after he died.

In the night, desperate with a heavy torch,
she clawed at the damp ground, sobbing.

Her mother suggested cutting up his shirts
to use for dusters. She took an afternoon off work,

piled the shades of Egyptian cotton at her feet.
Slicing away the arms, she began to fillet large squares

of cloth, smoothing them flat on the kitchen table.
A patchwork of arguments, dinner parties, sex

spread before her. A story for each shirt
but the pale blue *Ralph Lauren* bought for his thirtieth

was missing. He wore it that day, getting into the car,
the sun causing him to narrow his eyes as he waved

leaning from the window, promising to call her when he got there.

AEROPLANES

I like to think, when the bomb went off
she slipped from her seat
into the sky, floated for a time
before the body broke apart.
It's difficult to keep her whole.

Now that this package has come,
(her things wrapped in plastic)
I worry they were carelessly scooped up.
That I will tear away the wrapping
to find her fingers, loose, like crayons.

Night of the news flash, I sat on the stairs,
absolutely sure she had survived.
I kept my runway of Christmas lights
blinking on the banister for weeks,
but she didn't make it home.

I'd signed for my daughter's things,
went to work, left them untouched in the hall.
Opening my front door now, a stench hovers.
Diesel fuel, instantly thick in my throat,
with the hang of disinfectant behind.

The package mocks me, it's what I've waited for,
but I find it choking, unpleasant.
I lift it to the garden, let the smell seep upwards,
hear the rumble of distant aeroplanes.
Eagerly I look for her.

The long, hard legs puncturing clouds
as she falls down to me.
My hands getting ready to grab the feet,
pull her safely through the trees.

Beverley Gray

VILLANELLE: DEATH BY WATER

Towards its end my life has sped too fast,
and all the lessons learnt condense to one –
that I must lie by water at the last.

In spring I missed the tide before the mast:
as gibing boats in heavy weather run,
towards its end my life has sped too fast.

In college, though I worked, I was outclassed
by others sprawling in the summer sun.
Just let me lie by water at the last.

For social games I always felt miscast,
and though through autumn gales some friends I've won,
towards its end my life has sped too fast.

When winter flays bent willows in its blast
I welcome floods and meadows over-run,
for I must lie by water at the last.

There were a few successes in the past,
but more regrets for plans still left undone.
Towards its end my life has sped too fast,
now let me die by water at the last.

Philip Gross

BURNED OUT

                on the edge of the village:
a bungalow, the old body's who draped a damp
Jubilee teacloth on the one gas heater
in the one room she'd retreated to
                and no,

        the agent puts in, quick, (who wants a home
        brushed by that dark wing) she lived. Though
        who'd have wished her back to see it,
                peeled crusts

of green paint blow-torched
from the frames; an up-shadow
of soot from every window;
fissured chunks of charcoal joists;
                a buckled

        PVC back door in situ,
        with the handle-lock fused shut?
        Steep years of bramble-wilderment
                behind. But

now the builders float, pass to and fro
at ceiling height, on planks, above
the raked-out husk, a whole new storey
growing where she might have, for
                a moment, looked

        up as the smoke rolled back, the ceiling
        furled itself away...and seen them
        (they say she was wandering, getting lost
                in time):

Shadrach, Meshach, Abednego
in overalls, with tool bags – silent soon-
to-be men glowing in the updraught, on the tightrope
of the future, through the furnace,
                    not consumed.

GLOSA: WESTRON WYNDE

(for J. K. Gross 1919-2011)

Westron wynde, when wilt thou blow,
The small rains down can rain -
Cryste, that my love were in my armes
And I in my bedde again!
                    (Anon., medieval)

Where were we? Something shifted in the night,
as if the house resettled – ground
easing itself with a groan…. If not
the house, then maybe weather. The wind
still held its … not quite a note,
rather, a space into which a note might go,
live and not matter, like the sound of sand
that travellers' tales called *singing.* Infinite
distance but close, like that nobody's song: *oh*
westron wynde, when wilt thou blow …

Where are you now, who couldn't hold a tune
or the country of singers you left? You'd no choice
about that, any more than for me, my tone-
deaf smudges on the air that no advice
or scolding at the age of ten
could school. No choice but *play it again,*
for us both, that shared halt in the voice
on the phone or off guard. It's my turn
to hear its crackle at the windowpane:
The small rains down can rain.

That's not your language or your kind of song,
or not in public. *Tears, idle tears...?*
Give me patience! you'd say. Give tongue
to rage, grief or repining, they take liberties,
and homes, and lives. One must be strong.
You were – outliving friends and false alarms,
heart pills and hospital calls, for thirty years,
eventually alone...where you seemed to belong,
not free from but at home with harm.
Cryste, that my love were in my arms

though who or what your *love* might signify,
buried in languages she could not speak,
my mother soon learned not to pry.
A wind from somewhere colder, it might leak
through the cracks in your voice, as now in mine.
Leave it to music, or to silence, to explain
what words would make too rigid and too weak.
The wind has shifted; so we redefine
our foursquare walls by what they can't contain.

You, gone. And I ... *I in my bedde again.*

A LOVE SONG OF CARBON
(for JKG and MJAG 10.06.12)

For six years, on a high shelf in an upstairs bedroom,
    she was the only one who did not change.

Down here, in the oxygen economy, we came and went,
    our carbon still mixed with water, breathing, moistening,
        drying – yes, even our youngest, there, etching in breath

on the glass, now a smiley or down-in-the-mouth-now
    moon-face dripping. *He* took time, the eldest, withering

without her, needing ointments for his thinned
     and flaking skin – the sores on his shin did the weeping,
         the chemical bonds coming loose, letting parts of him go…

As patient as she'd learned to be in life, she
     waited, dressed and contained – in leather-textured

cardboard round a screw-top urn. Six years till the day
     they could meet in all simplicity, at last, entirely
         conversant with each other. Ash into ash

lifts from my broadcast scatter, and into a wet wind
     for winnowing, chalkier flakes dropping free

into wire-rooted ling, small gorse, bell heather,
     rabbit scuts; the finer grains fetched up (we
         flinch, then stay, yes, why not let them dust us)

lifting towards Sheepstor, North Hessary Tor,
     Great Mis Tor and the deeper moor beyond

whatever the skyline he and she had ever reached.
     The rain clouds come up over Cornwall like the grey
         Atlantic. Generations. Wave on wave on wave.

June Hall

BATH-TIME

Gran was bulk, padding, rough tweed
to my mother's pink silk and ballerina froth.
She was a church-going woman, duty

stitched into her hems, polished into post-war
brogues and darned with large sampler stitches
into navy cardigan and thick beige stockings.

Hers weren't the arms I wanted as I wept
(Mum already half way to London to try her luck
at the single life), but she rubbed kind words

into me with a loofah, soaped me with rhymes,
planted me on the wide acreage of her lap;
wedged between broad-bank thighs. I let her

bury me in layers of rough white bath towel
like a milk-tooth folded deep in a grown-up hanky,
hiding its tiny, blood-stained stump.

BOWING TO WINTER

White infant-coffin with grown-up silver name-plate;
breasts that leaked and dribbled, un-sucked;
a need crying in every nerve – yet for all this,

nothing could make your heart beat again or put the leaves
back on the November branches or, with the turn of the month,
make the hanging of Christmas holly bearable.

Like sweets in wartime, though, I hoarded

scores of unexpected letters, rationing myself to one a day.
I never knew I had so many weeks of friendship –

I bow to them now: to the surgeon who cried delivering you;
the nurses who took your picture and lifted you into
your father's arms, he, stooping to gather you;

bow to an ending that preceded a beginning;
to the cold time of not-knowing, the barren place of waiting,
bow to winter – and to rare flashes of spring.

DEAD AND ALIVE

I am thirst of the desert
I am sting of the sand-cloud,

the hopeless hunch
of weeping breath, gritted eyes.

Milk bleeds from heavy breasts,
burns dry on useless nipples;

arms reach to hold the mirage,
cramp at the never-will-be weight.

Without life, nothing to give.
I am human coffin, I am body-box.

Inside, lies – my son.

ANNIVERSARY

November reaches bare-boned to the sky,
branches splayed like starving arms,
a withered straggle of leaves
flagged against the morning mist.

Month of mud and worn-out grass,
stone-cold waiting and silent poppies,
Day of the Dead. A crimson teardrop
hangs from the nose of the stillborn son

I stroke but never hold, scared
his paper skin will flake, twig limbs
melt like snow – summer's growth
all broken up. The years flow back to

that November when, unsuspecting,
my stripped-down heart, bared
to the bleak helplessness of love,
riots with unseasonal blossom.

81 VICTORIA DRIVE
(for Judith)

Your buttercup kitchen, its brightness
cluttered with toys from the attic, is where
you used to start the day: brewed coffee, got cross,
quelled the grandchildren and their minor mutinies
where you argued the toss, read the paper, giggled
and, always ready to help, planned strategies.
But this kitchen's empty – nothing starts here now –
except the day.

The sitting-room, smelling of mahogany-polish
and open fires, waits for a date to entertain.

The curtains must have been swished shut.
Is that you lingering at the piano,
fingers tiptoeing across the keyboard?
Is that your rusty voice, soaring then falling
into rhythms of ragtime laughter? In the half-light
shadows reach across

into the hall, where, with its warm wrap
of overcoats, open visitors' book and spare keys,
you always gave us your best hello-hug;
now it's chilly: all chair-lift, burglar alarm
and drifts of undirected letters on the stairs
while your grandfather clock waits to be wound.
That's not you at the front door, is it, letting rip
about the dust, not

YELLOW BIRD
(Inspired by *Yellow Bird,* a pastel by Hugo Colville)

Out of a hole in the man's chest pops a bird,
flags in the sag of the torso a hollow round the heart
where smart surgeons have jig-sawed and cut away
so the tin man goes on ageing when rage bends him
squared in on himself, shoulder and elbow bent.
His cornered body, once upright and steel-strong,
now light with emptiness, is grown grey, suit-coloured,
its geometric planes drawn in pain.... And yet

hunched, one-legged in his own shadow,
he cranes to the bird's bright wink, chin pegged
to his shoulder, a thin cushion for the night
when the flight of the yellow bird is unseen so
no-one knows where it's been till it opens its beak
and speaks secrets that range beyond tears and grief
to a comfort that's strange as a bird on the wing for a man
clamped in a square tin can, sealed in a vacuum... And yet

THE TRUTH TRAIL

She tells us not to fuss –
why's she fussing then?
It's only an old shake.
Adults are so sad!

What should I tell him?
The truth is like a tight-tied sack
whose canvas frays around the seams
and leaks a trail of tell-tale dust.
His finger hesitates to trace
black question marks in what is spilt.

It's nothing, is it?
Though I've heard her on the phone
talking like it was.
What is it she won't tell?

Shouldering alone
the unknown contents of the sack,
I fear its weight would flatten him.
And so I measure out the truth
in tiny less alarming heaps.
He piles them up but doesn't speak.

UNTIMELY

A rope tightens rough around my chest
as I breathe in my bare-topped children,
brush their summer skin, smell their smallness.

Willow arms trail sleep across the bed,
fingers floating towards his teddy. Beside him
his twiggy sister sprawls, drooped on an edge.

These long-limbed saplings need me
firm-rooted and, as in this vigil, still – not
quivering, shaken with disease, old too soon.

The time is out of synch like a match
that burns too fast, searing fingers
when the flame goes out, candles not yet lit.

Katherine Hall

HOME

Poetry locked in pain,
as even your words imitate
the stony grit of teeth
and soft, shuddering steps.

Bambi on ice,
a careless youthful memory
flickers then dies.
Childhood has no place now.

Circling the subject,
we dismiss the 'what ifs?'
Father and daughter polished with denial,
yet carved from solid oak.

The house echoes our noise,
shelters memories in the welcoming walls
and clings to you,
with its crooked curves.

Gently,
they weave a path through the hurt,

fill the gaps where words should go.
With lumped throat I watch
the two-man army, proudly bearing

their upturned tails: raised flags of hope.

B
R   O   K
        E N

Miss and love and where are you
who it is and why and what and how
How could you and did you mean it
and I don't know what to say
and nor do you
and love and lies and lies and lies.
Broken promises and a future planned
that never meant much
outside of adjectives. Do you
remember when and happy
and used to be and changed
and sorry I'm not the way I was
with cruelty and anger and never forgotten.
Clinging on to dreams, memories,
laughter, tears
and tears and tears.
An eye for an eye they said
we made it a break for a break.
Broken words we never meant
and broken promises we never kept.
Ended and over and empty and silence
and cracks and splits and nothing
and pain and pain and pain
and I still don't know what to say.

Pasting the cracks with someone
else, moving on and new chapters.
Love and Loss and Loss of Love
and space and quiet and peace
and I don't recognise you any more
and past is past and past is gone.
Time. Stopped. Then starts and suddenly
the days tick past. A new clock,
with gentle hands. They circle and
swerve and revolve around
a new me. Forgotten us.
Broken-limbed, heavy with pain
and done, and done and done.

Richard Hall

A FAMILY *WHY?*

When you're gone
I'll think of you,
see you sitting there
bound by that constant posture:
spindly limbs and nervous looks,
smiles,
caring words and un-aired doubts

(shame about the house!
 ... But the garden's nice)

How could I ever forget
those times when I was closer
and you, strong and loving,
tall with the keen auburn purpose
of that generation that did its duty,

would handle my barrage of *whys*
through doubt-filled certainty.

Your wilderness taught you gratitude
and us to appreciate
the joy in routine,
days out, frail hugs
and questioning gossip.

Granny's here!
And that's how I'll see you,
riding that wave of certainty
your routine rising up over us
even after I outgrew it.

You – that fine balance
More *whys* than you might admit to.
Expectant on the horizon,
forever stayed by that dent that love leaves,
you'll never be forgotten.

Ruth Hanchett

NO PASSING BY

Her face is white, yellow,
grey – like the wintry day –
skin as parchment, tight
over her cheekbones.

The path is narrow –
no chance of passing by.
Widow for a week. What
can one say? Then,

How's it going? Up and down.
Signal to listen – to catch
the moment, seek its centre,
try to caress the cold.

LOOSENING

Tight inside
the knot of grief
is straining.

Clumsy fingers
try to unpick their way
into a parcel

marked *fragile*
boxing in
the past order of things.

Touched
by other people's stories
of their lost routines

the knot then loosens
releases the past
to begin an escape

energises new lightness,
a flash of insight
and now

she can hurry home
rearrange the furniture
sort out his clothes.

Sophie Hannah

YOUR DAD DID WHAT?

Where they have been, if they have been away,
or what they've done at home, if they have not –
you make them write about the holiday.
One writes *My Dad did*. What? Your Dad did what?

That's not a sentence. Never mind the bell.
We stay behind until the work is done.
You count their words (you who can count and spell);
all the assignments are complete bar one

and though this boy seems bright, that one is his.
He says he's finished, doesn't want to add
anything, hands it in just as it is.
No change. *My Dad did*. What? What did his Dad?

You find the 'E' you gave him as you sort
through reams of what this girl did, what that lad did,
and read the line again, just one 'e' short:
This holiday was horrible. My Dad did.

Peter Hawkins

THE FINAL GIFT
(for Dad: April 2013)

Shortly before he died, I was sitting with my Father as he slept, and
suddenly he awoke, and said:
*Oh good, I am glad you are still here. I want you and Michael to both have
one of my sticks, so when you are old men you can use it in the garden and
think of me. Please take it with you.* I took the stick and thanked him,
and as he fell back into sleep I wrote this poem.

Take my stick
For I have walked this path before you
Let my path and stick guide your way.

The path is slow and winding
The challenges sometimes blinding
When your feet begin their sliding
But your soul still finds the way.

Take my stick,
For my hand can no longer hold you,
My voice no longer guide you,
My eyes no longer see you.

Once on the path behind me,
Now on the path before me,
Go on the path and be me,

The old man tapping,
His life slowly sapping,
The sea gently lapping
The old man has found his way.

Pippa Munro Hebden

YELLOW JACKET

I kept your bright yellow sailing jacket.
It was much too useful to give away.
Double-zipped and waterproof with a hood
It keeps me dry as I trudge through the fields.
I think of you pacing the wooden decks,
Your blue eyes scrunched against the salty wind,
Flapping sheets of canvas above your head,
The rigging snapping and the prow dipping.
My seas are grass tracks with sandbanks of mud.
A black leather leash lies coiled in my hand.
A tall butterscotch hound pads silently
Behind me, just as you always used to do:
I turn around to check that she's still there.
I caress her fur, softer than your beard.
Her chestnut eyes are puzzled by my tears.
I thrust my hand deep into one pocket.
Your folded handkerchief is always there.

Marianne Hellwig John

DUST

A film of dust
obscures memories,
like the clay dust
in her studio
which glittered in light
layered all surfaces.

I hated the grit,
the lethal powdering,

though I loved to see
her kneading clay, till
from her busy fingers
gradually life appeared.

Dust took her life –
her enemy silicosis –
not Himmler's men
from whom she had fled.
At the end, her wasted fingers
shrank from the touch of clay.

Diana Hendry

DRESSING MOTHER

I help roll her stockings over her feet,
then up to her knees. She's managed her dress
but I free her fingers from the sleeves.
Before the mirror she rouges her cheeks,
combs her thin curls, hands me a bow.
It's scarlet and goes on a ribbon I thread
under her collar and fix with a hook.
Over an hour to dress her today.

Such an innocence stays at the nape of the neck
it fumbles my fingers. I see her binding
bands of scarlet at the ends of my plaits
and fastening the buttons at my back.
Now look – she's dressed as a child off
to some party. I straighten her scarlet bow

and don't want her to go,
don't want her to go.

Michael Henry

FUNERAL KISS

A custom, I thought, more honoured
in the breach than in the observance.
A custom for Russian presidents lying in state.
A custom for the bones of the beatified
whose very deadness might spark some life.

I wanted to isolate you in the privacy
of death and said *No* to Mrs Taetz,
our children's carer, who asked to pay her respects
and *No* to Les Corness who asked
if he could take photographs of you dead.

I viewed you but didn't want to kiss you.
I didn't want to feel the *Ding an sich* of death
as if that final funeral kiss
might undo all those other kisses:
before, during, after, first, best.
And yet now I feel I should have kissed you,
a tiny peck perhaps, a tiny brush with death
to show I was your brave boy grown into a man.

Gaia Holmes

ALL I CAN DO FOR YOU IS DREAM...

I know you'll be awake now.
You'll be out in the garden shed
as far away as you can get
from the house and its damp wreaths,
its stink of grief and lilies.
You'll be sitting amongst
plant pots, pegs and windfall apples
smoking cigarettes.

Here the street is sleeping.
I skulk around the kitchen
in the dull fridge light, avert my eyes
and tiptoe past the pink sloe gin.

I could drink now.
I could drink for me, for you,
for the whole of the island.
I could drink for remembrance,
knock back a teacup for all the dead souls
searching for that bright crack back into life.
I could drink now but it's 4am
and I've got an empty bed to fill
and dreams to dream for both of us.

PENINSULA

You walk it like a tightrope,
broad feet turned out, balancing your way
along the skinny peninsula.
This is the penultimate side-show,
your dextrous circus trick.

I'd rather there was this link between us,
this bony joint of sand and grass
than the distance of you
on your dog-eared island
drifting further and further away.
Your letters are rare now.
You send me dislocated objects:
chips of lustre
hacked from oyster clasps,
fat lenses of jelly fish
packed in jigsaws of ice,
fossils that thud through the door
and crack on the white porch tiles
revealing histories
that have nothing to do
with you and me.
And lately you have been sending
razor shells and cuttle bones
things too sharp for remembrance,
pictures of your house
sinking back into the sea,
your name dissolving
as the ink runs dry.

Joy Howard

EMPTY

Houses need to be lived in –
yours, empty for a year,
is showing its displeasure.

Wallpaper droops
from the ceiling – a dozen
small flies in cobweb shrouds
shadow windows.

There's not much dust
no living thing to feed it –
likewise the dehumidifier
no longer whirrs.

Detritus, still unsorted
reproachful of the hand
that has stopped clearing
lies in unchanging heaps.

My hand, your house
both missing you
both empty of life.

TRAVELLING NORTH
(for my mother)

It came to me
at Hawick   in the
border country

Doing what I always
do   on holiday

at a pit-stop   head
for a CD   a book
a present
for someone

This is a mill town
here is the mill
there are the jumpers   the
cashmere   the soft
the pretty   and here
am I   with tear-water turning
the heart like an old
mill wheel

I want to buy you
a jumper
and you'll never be glad
of one   of me
again

All week running
in the wild race
of mourning   now sinking
like a stone thrown
into a mill pond
You're gone
and I'm
in another land

TWO YEARS ON

Through the disconsolate rain
of a grey northern town
I search for you

I walk past the funeral parlour
my final blurred sighting
laying my last gifts beside
the you that was no longer you

I drive our old route to the hills
avoid the hospital – pointlessly –
as memory direct and sharp as a pen
writes hard and clear

I sit in your room observe
your collection of glass on the sill
pooling grey light into brightness
summoning me into Spring

I find you there

Frieda Hughes

FOR NICK

The sun rises and sets
In spite of our absence,
Oblivious of our separation by death
Or your part in my evolution.
But your shadow remains
As if you never left; it's mine now.

I would never have given you up
Except that you were borrowed;
To be returned to the primal clay.
Had I known that each day
Counted you off like fingers
I might have mourned sooner

The idea of impending loss.
It would have eroded
The years I thought we'd share;
That necessary ignorance was bliss
Reassuring me that nothing was amiss.

But you remain alive for me;
I hear you speak as you commit
The mundane actions of a day; you eat; you sleep;
You exist – an echo from the walls
Of every room I occupy.
The recollection of your voice
Plucks at the sinews of the instrument
I have become for you. That music
Argues with the loss of presence
That your ashes signify;
and our sibling shadows dance.

Nora Hughes

STEAM

His cough scuffs the bedroom wall.
I lie awake listening, my blood

darkens to steel. *If I'm*
for the high-jump ..., he says

in the morning in the sun–
filled kitchen, where steam

spirals up from the curved spout
of the tin teapot, wraps itself

around his head.
He stirs her tea. *I'll take this up*

to your mother. In the draught
of the closing door, steam tumbles.

DESERT

My father told me how darkness comes in the desert
with blades of cold, how the soldiers huddle together,
their mouths burning, how moonlit bones shine
through their dreams all night.

                    Now a voice crackles
in the phone – he's calling me – through the tangle of static
I hear sand grains spinning in the wind, his breath
gusting along a line so fine it wavers
in and out of being. Words reach me
one by one – *wind   bones   home* –
they lodge themselves in my throat.

                    The crackle stops.
I tap out messages with long attachments
till the room grows dim.

                    Every day
he calls me from the desert, on an old phone
clogged with sand, where bones flicker through the
filmy dark, and the cold shows no mercy.

Rosie Jackson

HAVING IT ALL

Already you have half disappeared
your limbs as thin as broom handles.

You sent me off to Tuscany
so you could shrink in silence
wanting me to live the life
you dreamt other people had

but still I am the daughter of your austerity
caught in your habits of the Blitz
long after any real war was done.

I never saw you crease in laughter
enjoy a ribald joke
tuck into fattening food
drink more than a bird's sip
of sherry.

And now you are propped
on your hospital bed
listening with deaf ears
to your favourite myth
that the meek will inherit the earth.

How I want for you a different ending

to see you rise like yeast
in the bread you used to knead
full of zest, sap, juice, joy, certainty;
to have you shake your shoulders free,
stand tall and, with no apology,

looking neither back nor down
jump with both feet and claim it all:

the radiance
the stars

the full-fat light.

MY MOTHER'S ENGAGEMENT RING

Handed to me in a plastic bag
along with cash and wedding ring
this solitaire diamond

the tiny holes around the mount
which hold the diamond proud
clogged now with sediment.

For hours I scrub
with my inter-dental brush
prodding out the years

of standing at the sink,
the silt of soil, of soap,
of thread, of pastry dough,

tissues, hand-cream, widowhood,
thinking of all the things she touched
those last forty years

and all the things –
a man, a child, a glass of wine –
she didn't.

THE LETTER CUTTER

You have carved them
so many times
these dates that sit before and after a life.

You know the best texts,
the forms, the letters sans serif,
unyielding capitals.

You have stood so often
on this threshold
of the other world

like an Egyptian bird,
broad-shouldered, dark,
you must know something of the mystery,

something of what remains
of a man beyond
these ceremonial bookends.

Day after day you hammer
home the stone
to just the right depth

in just the right spot
for these characters of love
to catch the light.

Jennifer Johnson

MISSING

I miss the room
you allowed me
to stretch out in;
you who knew
what I liked to eat,
which places
were special to me.

Now I feel squeezed
into a corridor
with my cases,
tired of having nowhere
to put out my things,
of repeating
the basic facts.

If only I could,
once again,
talk with someone
who already knows
the pictures
I would like to put
on my walls.

Hilary Jupp

MOTHER ORCHARD COTEHELE

I walked through Mother Orchard,
passing saplings, half my height,
inspecting their bracelets of identity – Sawpit,
Snell's Glass Apple, Honeypinnick – infant trees,
refugees once grubbed out from these valleys.

I turned north, looking over fields,
fresh ploughed, toward the mound of granite heath,
Kit Hill. When, as if drawn by the sweet sting
of apple on the tongue,
my mother came to me.

Linking arms we strolled along,
pausing for a smile with Pollywhitehair,
with Cornish Gillyflower, thriving youngsters,
who in the years to come will mature, bear fruit,
donate grafts, mother their own apple saplings.

Jackie Kay

THE BIRD
(i.m. Julia Darling)

Coming in, only now, as if released like that bird,
the story of the bird,
as if something earlier, the cold hands of grief
had double-locked the door and put on the chain.
Yet now the back door is miraculously open:
you are up, surprised to be walking again

into this cottage, a mug of tea in your hand.
Since you've been gone, you've become a grandmother.
Something strange happened to time:
it got longer, and shorter; it was numbered. Numb.
And when once it hurt to think of you dead

now you move at ease around in my head.

THE NO-LONGER DEAD

The people who are no longer dead,
who were so cold in their skin, so unlike their old selves,
have returned to the living rooms and kitchens
fields and gardens, beaches and benches,
streets, bus stops, cafés; all their favoured places.

How surprising it is, when you go to cut the hedge
or cut back the cherry blossom tree, or water the clematis,
or retile the roof, or buy from the deli some strong cheese –
how strange and pleased you are to find them coming too,
no longer gaunt; nothing left of that old disease.

Back, the long-ago-deceased, they've put weight on,
and are hanging around the old haunts,
having their open-ended conversation. You can even hear a laugh.
The voice you thought you had forgotten
has returned, with almost the same intonation.

Dear friends, you find yourself saying, *over the moon!*

Ann Kelley

A LUMP IN THE THROAT

This lump in my throat
is a stone I cannot swallow:
it stops my breath my speech
all my tomorrows.

I should wield a white stick
wear a widow's weeds or at least
a black armband, a plaster cast,
bruises purple and yellow

or have one of those sexy bandages
around my naked shoulder and torso
like a shot cowboy hero. If I wore
dark glasses they would see I am blinded.

If I wore a hearing aid they would shout through the sorrow.
I will drown in shallow water, my heart is hollow.

TELLING THE BEES★

I had to tell the cats
Like telling the bees.
They knew, anyway,
But saying the words made it real.

The large tabby lowered his head
And with it comforted my hand.

★*An old English tradition, after a death, to stop bees leaving the hive*

FLUENT

He is a man who forgets who his wife is,
most of the time he's off with the fairies.

He's mislaid the name of his home
and like a faded dream several languages have gone.

He's lost the trick of spreading cut halves
of a scone with jam and cream.

He's a man who forgets he has a nose
that needs blowing and wiping,

but when the jazz starts playing
he gets up and bebops, fluent feet remembering.

Lisa Kelly

DEATH CERTIFICATE, BURNT OAK

Dealing with the paperwork of dying,
the registrar looks dead bored, and, sighing,
he asks for my dad's place and date of death
and birth, job, names, and last usual address.
As he writes it down, his signet ring gleams
on his little finger. He looks up, leans
towards my mother, and his pen is poised,
as he asks her, as wife of the deceased,
her name, and, at last, her occupation.
Housewife, she says. A hesitation,
he wrinkles his brow, and, again, he sighs,
taps his pen. *Is that all? Yes,* she replies,
and in her voice, there's no hint of recoil,
while I said nothing, but boiled. And still boil.

FOR SALE

This house has no history, nothing to sweep away, no broom.
The walls are white, floors washed. No one died in the living room
lying on a loaned hospital bed, attached to a morphine drip.
There was no swab with a pink-tipped sponge to wipe on cracked lips.
There were no chairs pulled untidily around, no wine in glass,
no sentimental music played, just in case hearing is the last
sense to leave. No doctor called to confirm death at…
I forget. No body left this house in a bag. That
never happened. And the hands on that body in that bag,
never took out groceries from a shopping bag,
glad to be home after the crowds, glad to peel
potatoes, scrub carrots, baste meat for a family meal.
They never opened the door, welcomed in, covered a cough,
washed grandchildren, washed-up, wiped down, waved off.
No, this house has no history. No husband nursed by his wife,
both gone. It has blank walls on which you can write your life.
It has no furniture left, no squashy sofa, scratched dining table,
children's framed scribbles, to clutter your view of its potential.
It has no curtains because it has nothing to hide.
The estate agent said this house will go easily. He lied.

HOMEWARD BOUND

I forget their names. Peter and Paul perhaps,
definitely not Burke and Hare. Well-mannered,
no distinguishing features. Salt-of-the-earth chaps.
Gentle when they lifted my mother on to the trolley bed.
Wheeling her away they were careful of corners,
conscious that her bones hurt,
easing her fears with solicitous murmurs,
There, Lilian. Home soon. Nothing more to avert.
Goodbye to the nurses who had done so much,
remembering gown, comb. Goodbye to hope.
On with the journey. Only our fingers touch,

wanting to reassure within this limited scope.
Inside this ambulance, we each have a view:
a traffic jam for them; home for her; for me a pew.

Mimi Khalvati

PRUNUS AVIUM

We buried my mother's ashes in the holes, the four
we dug to plant four cherry trees for her, *prunus avium:*

wild cherry, sweet cherry, bird cherry, gean or mazzard,
each name carrying something of *prunus avium* on the wind,

the wind that blew drifts of ash like bonemeal across clay.
In three years they'll be grown; in twenty, diamond woodland.

But we'll recognise our trees, set back where the path ends.
Surrounding them will be native oak, beech, alder, hazel.

One cherry tree from each of us: Tara, Bea, Kai and myself.
And on Tom's behalf, we invoked the name of Yax Tum Bak,

Mayan God of Planting, there in a desolate, bitterly windy field
in Buckinghamshire. Clay stuck to our boots in grassy clumps

and as Tara heaved her spade, worms, lustrous as white mulberries,
fled, upturned. Later, in the Garden Centre – *Oh, how beautiful!*

my mother would have gasped on entering – I bought Tara
a peach tree for Valentine's Day, *Prunus Persica,* from Persia.

TEARS

In the first weeks after my mother's death,
I curled up on the side of my heart like a foetus

and wept. My tears were like water, sweet and clear.
They flowed of their own accord, soundlessly,

while my body, my mouth and even my eyelids
lay as peacefully as in sleep and the more tears flowed,

the more I wanted them. World was foetal then.
But in the months that followed, tears dried up

and the world took up its stick and walked blindly
through the riverbeds. Had they been floodplains,

had there been no dams to render them obsolete,
milometers would have measured the overflow

from faraway monsoons on stairs, pillars, wells.
Too high and there'd be famine, too low, the same.

I measured distances by her. My mother my compass,
my almanac and sundial, drawing me arcs in space.

WHAT IT WAS

It was the pool and the blue umbrellas,
blue awning. It was the blue and white

life-size chess set on the terrace, wall of jasmine.
It was the persimmon and palm side by side

like two wise prophets and the view that dipped
then rose, the swallows that turned the valley.

It was the machinery of the old olive press,
the silences and the voices in them calling.

It was the water talking. It was the woman
reading with her head propped, wearing glasses,

the logpile under the overhanging staircase,
mist and mountains we took for granted.

It was the blue-humped hose and living wasps
swimming on the surface. It was the chimneys.

It was sleep. It was not having a mother,
neither father nor mother to comfort me.

John Killick

THE SCATTERING

Yesterday we said
if it's fine we can set her free
to float in the sunlight,
but today we can't see our way.

Death perhaps, is no more
than a kind of scattering
into a field of mist
behind which the sun shines.

CENTRAL

This is a terminus,
turning-point for lives, and I
am standing in the middle
of the concourse, crowds milling
around me...which way to go?
I start off in a direction,
people part to let me through,
and begin to recognise faces.
I know that one but can't place
exactly where we met.
This one's familiar too,
and goes back a long way,
to schooldays and beyond.
They greet me, smile, exchange
a few words, clasp hands,
then melt away. So many...
not all a pleasure to see:
here's a teacher gave me strokes,
another strokes of a different kind.
There's a librarian I loved,
a housekeeper who found me kind.

I approach a barrier...
I don't seem to know this line.
But who do I find standing there
but you, quizzical, amazed,
as if to say: *so it's true*
on this part of the journey
you've found a companion.
We link arms and stride
out. There is no train,
the lettering on the destination
board's illegible, but
there's lots of strangers waiting.
They greet us as if they know us

as ourselves, and that feels good.
And now our perspective
narrows to the empty end
of the platform beyond
which lies the tunnel mouth.
We turn, embrace, I let go
of your hand, and wave, then
walk on into the dark.

ALMOST THROUGH

You seem already almost through
the door that opens for us all
but cannot tell me anything
of what lies on the opposite side…
closer, yet further away.

Your body speaks the lines
your mouth can no longer utter
and I am here to learn them.
Each posture, every gesture,
that glint in the eye, cry, turn down
of the mouth, pressure of the finger tips…
are not to be taken in isolation,
but make up a composite
of who you were and are.

So, before it's too late, may I
be your ghost-writer? Let's create
this last chapter together.

Wendy Klein

CLEARANCE

Table linen in neat piles, inset
with open-work lace and starched
stiff as sails in full wind,

and that it's raining

sixty years of books, including
a fifties' *Encyclopaedia Britannica*,
German titles in *Deutsche Schrift*,

a letter from a relative in New York
offering affidavits to the family
which saved some lives,

as the traffic outside gets heavier,
the tarmac dark with wet and swept
with the hiss of passing cars

and that it's still raining.

Family portraits of great-grandmothers –
both sides – coiffed, bombazined,
leg o'mutton sleeved; they glower

at this packing up, look set to protest
as the lamps that still have bulbs are lit
against the gloom inside,

the rain outside not letting up

the listing floor lamp,
the pair of matching Delfts,
their chipped bases,

the oval table, its fruitwood marquetry
defaced by the prints of careless drinkers;
you crying out, but refusing pain relief

and that it's raining, raining, raining.

Kaye Lee

NOT FOR US

Do we grow old? Our mothers did,
and our fathers, before we knew them,
but not us, not you and me,
for ever not quite mature.

Our brothers and sisters grew old,
left us behind; their children
are growing old – they've passed us
on that journey. We stay at the bus stop,
watch others board as we eat our sandwiches,
drop orange peel for the street sweeper
to sweep into his long-handled pan.

Another bus comes. Your father, my mother
beckon but we turn our backs
take out a thermos of half-cold coffee.
We'll stay here, we say, *let you
go ahead, make everything ready.*

and then

and then we will know
and be known more intimately
than a marriage
and yet always be
in the thrill of discovery
like Newton staring
at his apple, or Archimedes
dashing from his bath, *Eureka!*
stamped into each footprint
Peter crying: *You are the Christ!*

and we will always be
on the end page of our book
never having to read the closing
sentence or shut the book with a sigh
for lost friends

and we'll be forever printing out
the final version of our poem
knowing it will keep intact
its glow of perfection
each word, each space
where it must be

and then, when there is
no then, only now
we will be ourselves
unveiled, unreflected
totally real, wholly us
fit at last
to live

I want my mother, not her *chiffonier*
Fleur Adcock

How I wish I'd written that and sent it
to my mother though of course
it would not have been a chiffonier –
I doubt she'd ever heard the word
outside a puzzle. I could have said
the pair of china dogs, black and white
spaniels that sat patiently either end
the old mantelpiece, faithful guards
of the family photographs and trinkets
and only after she was gone I learned
my father chose them from a catalogue
as an unexpected gift and I could not
imagine my taciturn father showing
that amount of sentiment. Now the dogs
sit on our bookcase, their mouths shut tight
on the secrets of those lovers I never met,
can never know. Dear Mum and Dad,
I want to write, thank you for the dogs.
I care for them, keep them safe, try not
to blame them for regrets that fall
as black tears from their shiny eyes
to stain all my pictures of you.

Pam Leighton

HEART OF LOSS

Write in simple terms, my tutor said.
Keep to the facts. Give a reason
For every statement. Quote from the text.
Over the years I've learnt the ways
To score high marks in essays.

So I'll keep this simple too.
What comes next
Has much to do with Shakespeare
Who gave both love and death their season:
There was an ending.
You slipped away into another sphere
Suddenly. Joy and light went with you.

My understanding of this script is suspect.
Quotations do not exist. Reasons are few.
I do not expect
To score high marks.
Dark my days.

Loss unending

Tim Liardet

THE DARK AGE

By the time the second plane blew up
all he knew was he was one of a new race
entering a new age, in need of water:
the cloud of ash bulged between skyscrapers

that seemed to lean closer and he knew
his brother was there at the source of it –
so he stopped, he did the strangest thing,
he took off his railway-worker's coat

to improvise a street-bed, he thought of
unlacing his boots but recalled how a toe
poked through his sock-hole, then turned the coat
inside-out with the satin to the light

and rolled it up slowly, put his head
to the pillow he had made – his brother,
he knew, was at the source of the cloud
so he lay himself down exactly where he was

there in the street, tucked up his knees,
smiled, or wore a face that nothing could name,
then slept as the snowfall of ash, petal
for petal, covered him and everyone else.

THE REVENANT

This the door
opening from
the back of my neck
like a hatch
on a hinge:
(…you are such
a furtive, shifty
and insistent
ghost – you use
the hatch
like a cat-flap).
And this, brother,
your mewling
for food –
you expect
always to be
welcomed back,
while the flap
behind you
wipes out the last
of your tracks.
I must submit,
it seems,

to your taking
of death's steps
in reverse,
climbing the rungs
of my spine.
You climb so slyly,
so cagily,
as if to say:
where the ghost
comes to feed
through the hatch
there's a bowl.

LIKE SLANT RAIN

Trouble is with inventing a language, brother,
when the only other person in the world who speaks it dies
you're left speaking to no one. This mouthful of words

of fat verbs and vowels and cases and morphemes
that stammer from the lexicon under the tongue
is desperate to be used and anxious to be heard

and competes against itself for the room to speak –
it crowds out my mouth with the need to keep alive
every O in our intonation before it ends up

on the dump with the clicks of Hittite and Kulinic;
our words seem stranded and strangely marooned
now there's no one to read the other side of them.

No one to read them the wrong way round and still
have them make sense, say they are the wrong way round.
No one to say the old humanist's slanting hand

would not have wanted a mirror if he was the other side
but it's more necessary now, and I read in it:
lately, I confess, I've tried scrawling to myself in the glass

but, like any mirror-writing, it's slant rain. And like slant rain
it goes on falling and tearing, falling and tearing.
Like slant rain it quickens suddenly and slows down

and is heedless of its own expenditure.
Like slant rain it goes on falling and tearing, falling and tearing
and the glass does not know what it sees.

Maxine Linnell

ONLY YOU

'*T'sonly me*, sung through the phone,
you – who could never be only you –
who could be only and more than part of me
apart from, away from '*t'sonly you*
and when I said *how are you* –
as you do – and when I said
how are you, only you,
you said you're getting there –
and I repeated – *getting there* –
almost close enough down the phone
but not quite close enough,
getting there – wherever there is,
sometimes I said – *wherever that is, there,*

and I know you were getting there
– you are – because there is no there
or no there, then, before now.
And now you were there – then – you were there
when there was nowhere else to be.

VIGIL

I didn't know there'd be an after you –
there was before, before you
squirmed through your birth and
crashed me into motherhood.
Now there's a new before,
a new unwanted after
these six long months since.

Teachers named you a terrier.
You worried at big life questions
put nothing down until
fully examined and understood,
then bounded to the next.

That restlessness has stilled.
Your voice on the phone
– *'t'sonly me* – has gone.
You took most of me with you
in that moment slipped
between before and after.

Life lengthens, renews
itself not caring where,
blind to these longest nights
when vigil is not a choice.

BRICK LANE

You moved into Brick Lane,
that industrial room, pipes and wires exposed,
your hopes intact, promises piled
in stacked boxes lining the walls.

You could cycle round that room
it's so vast, and you did,
crowing with homeliness
and your smiling life.

Six months on you have gone.
We stack the boxes again.
Now they are loaded with tears.
They sag and teeter.

The evening sun sets light to dust in the air.
Dreams litter the floor. We sweep them away
into black bags, sweep till it's over.
Hand back the keys.

DAY

Waking to you dead each day
I have to find a way down
the lengths of day corridor
without adding bruises to bruises
without knocking at scabs
bleeding in too many places.
Hard when the floor lurches underfoot
bucks at every step.

DREAM

I dreamed of him
standing a few yards away
under a shower. He turned,
smiled at me briefly.
I went back to my car.
All the wheels had been taken.

AND NOW HE IS

The birthing tongs
doing what being might have done
in its own time
have marked their metallic shape
on his still-sliding skull plates.
He's bruised from out to in
and when he finds our world
he lets us know
how hard his way has been.
He seems too tender to touch
even to whisper a welcome.
He might break at a smile.
The midwife picks him up like porcelain
her hand fits round his hurting head.
He's beautiful, she says,
and now he is.

Deric Longden & Aileen Armitage

TO AILEEN

(by Deric for Aileen)

I love you because you take my heart
places where it has never been,
where it's easy to find my smile,
and I'm the best *me*
I have ever been.

You take me to a place where hope shines
more brightly for tomorrow,
and make me more at home
than I have ever known.

SUMMER STORM
(by Aileen for Deric 1936-2013)

Love like a summer storm fades
at last to evening calm
when the fierce reds and blacks
of passion, that rage at noon, cool
to pastel shades of tenderness,
and violent brush strokes slow
to a gently laying on of twilight.

The heat now gone,
gives way to gentler love.
It is sweeter so.

Bernard Lord

ALMOST TOMORROW

I'm at the outer
limits

reality is too much
the sunsets sensational
flowers blaze rainbows
seas roller-coasting
zinc white spray
in a cerulean sky

I'm on the outside
left the fold gone eyeing
you eyeing me
almost spirit

still here living
a grief

Janet Loverseed

THE LONELY AND THE SEA

We don't sleep well, we who have been left alone.
Fearing intruders, we lie stiff as bone
and listen to the creak of a floorboard,
a joist. We clench our teeth against a world
deemed hostile. But then, trying to relax,
we concentrate on safe sounds: rain, or the clicks
of the battery clock; we put our tongues
behind our top teeth to release our jaws;
we switch the radio on for company;
we get up at four to make tea.

Some of us, feeling lost in large houses,
move to smaller ones near our families,
or near our best friends, or in the country,
or closer to the town, or by the sea.
And maybe this last is just what we're seeking.
For won't the waves, in their rising and falling
and withdrawing their watery weight to rise
and fall again, and rise, and fall, and rise…
breathe like our old loves come back from the dead
to sleep beside us, here, in bed?

Rupert Loydell

NAMESAKE

My namesake killed himself with drink,
aunty had a massive stroke and died
just three weeks after burying uncle.

People disappear, lives change.
We no longer visit the places
where we have no reason to go.

If you don't travel there, then
memory goes away. Or fades,
like the photo beside our bed:

tin soldiers and model motorbikes
displayed behind your lovely smiles
in the house you had to move from.

Skirting depression's black hole
I long for childhood certainties,
time travel's impossible appeal.

But here we are in a small city
getting kids off to school in the rain,
trying to find time to be alive.

FURTHER THAN WE THOUGHT

We tried to make death look easy
a loss threaded through us.
Nothing, essentially, is forgotten
but silence is easier than memory.

Despite my faith in salvage
I will soon be running out of words.
We walked on the beach afterwards,
couldn't face the open grave.

Everyone was welcome back at the house,
so we went for tea and said goodbye.
It was further than we thought to home
and when we got there, difficult to stay.

Lachlan Mackinnon

IN MEMORY OF KEITH DARVILL
(1940-2008)

I
I could tell by the shelves of LPs
which house was yours; I didn't need the number
because their thin spines caught spare light
from the street; pale fishbone parallels.

You had said you were damned if at your age
you would become a morphine-addict.
You had a high pain-threshold
like my father.

At times your dark eyes
glittered, a trickster's,
and at times they were hazed
in reverie.

In the tipsy dawns
of your past, you had sometimes wept
at old songs ('Guantanamera'),
making conversation unnecessary.

Cooking, you were all clenched exuberance,
a pinch, a taste, a pinch, a taste
before you'd suddenly swoop the plates
down to your audience with your invariable *Eat!*

II
Everything's now too late.
In all our arguments
I was poetry, you
were stage and radio

and a true teacher,
furious on behalf
of films I hadn't seen,
music I hadn't heard,

which didn't just mean Bird
but Smetana,
Pete Seeger,
Jewish celebration songs.

Thanks to our ages,
this was the only friendship
of its kind I shall every make.
A joke along a bar

began it. Oh, the silences
men keep between them
when what they're keeping back
is what would spoil in being said.

SMALL HOURS

Somebody has been reading
Book of the Week
but the radio's off. I've heard the gale-warning
for the sea south of us.

              Rain
runs caressingly down the outside walls
of every room.

              Yesterday, two printed
death-announcements arrested me, the first
for a man rich in honours
who had made a hundred and one,

the second, right above it,
for a child who 'fell asleep' on her first day.

The rain quickens and falters, quickens.
Grief gusts around us
in stories we shall never know.

To report on the dreadful
with an unflinching voice,
is that poetry?
            To say
life is terrible, man a morass
of contradictions?
                Or to move
like a person of leisure, of dreamed-of leisure,
from long curtained rooms
to the bright thriving garden?
                    Ordered
as we would have it?
            Muse,
all you want is a few words
that will say how it was for us
at one a.m. on a Wednesday morning
so clearly that a thousand years may hear.

AT MARYCULTER

A stone cross on a double plinth gazes
across the valley. That white gable end
in a mist of stripped trees is the rented house
where my grandmother's childhood was so happy.

Bearing her ashes like an offering,
the minister climbs the track from the new manse.
His blue clerical shirt echoes the blue sky
of this freakishly bright December day.

The grave is open for the last time,
the family together. She has come home
or gone home. Let the winds blow on Maryculter,
let the snow snow on Maryculter:

when the memorials behind this granite
church of the Church of Scotland are long obscured
by the passage of many winters, I imagine some
passer-by stooping to wipe the moss off her name,

knowing nothing of all this, wondering.

Note: Maryculter is pronounced Marycooter

Gill McEvoy

WHEN GOD MADE TIME

I used to hate that phrase,
that *by the way* of yours
which meant we'd be the last to leave –

our hosts dancing on their toes,
hands on the door knob,
smiling through their teeth.

But your stories were so good...

Turn right, I'd say, navigating as you drove
and you'd go left
as if you couldn't bear to follow orders.
Only you could take an hour
to go three miles,
following one of your infallible short cuts.

I came to love that beech knoll
on the crest of Frankby Hill –
once, twice, three times around…

I gave you a watch: still you were always late.

When God made time he made plenty of it,
you laughed …

I'm the one left with all that time.

And I forgive you everything.

BREAD

It warms as I work it,
rocking heel to fingertip,
kneading it, letting it go.
The dough knits up the flour and salt,
stitching separate into whole.

I am considering
your death, my illness,
the burden of uncertain days.
I ball the springy globe tight,
stretch it like a rubber band, let it go.

It moulds itself into a mass
of yeasty muttering,
like men straining at a heavy task,
sweats and mumbles,
making something of itself. It grows

a mushroom sponge of hope.
I punch it down: it's mine to mould.

Joan McGavin

THE DRESSING-GOWN

Not to be shamed
by the old and tatty dressing-gown
she wore, for comfort,
in her own home –
here being public,
here the domain
of those who judge
by appearance –
urgent, in her hospital bed,
during that last illness,
she gave me an order.

Knowing her mindset
I bought the best I could:
quality above style
but colourful, completely lined
in cotton, *Made in England*.
We called it her
coat of many colours
and smiled with her
at how grand she looked.

Later, I wore it myself, sometimes,
on cold and sleepless nights.
It's been years.
Today, I've decided,
is the day I wrap it up
for the charity shop.
I know I can hand it over.
I know I'll be able
just to walk away
not to say

Give it a good home please:
some old lady
who's had a hard life,
like my mother's –
an old lady who wakes up cold.

Denise McSheehy

WHAT IS THERE TO BE AFRAID OF?

Only time, and time's
won out here, drawn his sting.

Today he's shambolic
lopsided, floppy-eared

nodding off as we talk –
All the things he didn't

do don't matter now.
And all the things he did.

Has his face shrunk, shrivelled
back to reveal the skull
teeth too big for his mouth
as if they'd startled.

He's on ahead – quicker than you thought
a loose runner, wall-

eyed and unpredictable
seeking the finish.

All the things he didn't do
All the things he did

HOW WOULD WE TALK?

Your yellow coat, the best sight
in the world. Your hands, the palms of your hands
seamed and tender. Their touch –

your dreaming face

The way you took your specs off
for close attention, eyes like blue lamps
suddenly huge.

Those solitary times before
three mirrors
the silver-backed brushes for your hair.

your dreaming face

How you smoked; fag in mouth
sorting sheets on wet Mondays
the kitchen steamy.
The piano's white keys
your hands, notes liquid and whole
informing my play on summer evenings.

your dreaming face

How when you weren't there, I was not –
lost, unfixed, looking for clues
smoke from the chimney, your bike at the gate.

The way you left, I forget.
Wind going through the house.
Hush

Ruth Marden

YES!

(for P.D. in tribute)

On the way to Athens airport almost, you announced
we'd time for the National Museum.
Why not? Why waste, you said,
a good half-morning? So we dodged
the traffic at Patission, and in your scrapbook still
The Little Jockey rides high.

On your way to the hospital appointment,
keyed up for sentence, you toured
Winchester Cathedral, listened attentively
to the guide. Gave the event due prominence
in your account of the day.

And on your way to your dying
you had so much to engage you. Old friends
to entertain, new ones to welcome in
your garden to be cherished and disciplined –
that shrub snicked to display
the three clematis blooms.
You wanted poetry read, your small radio
replaced. Thought of us all, tied up
every loose end. But kept us on our toes,
and sunlight held on, and still the shared
laughter.

Now you leave me
with time I must learn to fill.
Forgive me: it's jam-packed

with your absence.

Alwyn Marriage

LOST SCENTS

You saw the badgers just months before you died:
the satisfaction of a long-held dream
caught in our headlights, tumbling down the road;
and though the mellow cuckoo deep within the woods
eluded you, the skein of skylark song
emerged, just once, from background drone
to lift you briefly up in sheer delight.

But you had lost, irrevocably, your sense of smell,
would sniff frustratedly at flowers and lotions
then look around you accusingly as though
we hadn't shared a joke.
Nettles and flowering sea beet worked no magic
and even heady hyacinths in spring
couldn't pierce the blank. We wondered
whether aromatherapy might work;
if there was anything that could restore
olfactory satisfaction.

Now the question hinges on belief or fantasy.
Has cessation of your damaged mortal breath
released imprisoned scents?
It is possible
that joys restored are wafting over you
in a dimension I can no more see
now, than you could smell then.

UBUNTU LOVE SONG

I am because you are;
not just because we live
in a community of two,
but because the very breath I draw
is sweet and strong because it's shared
with you. Like everybody else, I am
a smattering of stardust down millennia,
a mixture of atoms and electric forces,
genes borrowed from many generations
now passed on.
But what am I without you?
A mouth unkissed, a body uncaressed;
the echo of a poem composed at night
then lost for ever in the morning's light.

Felicity Marris

THIS SUMMER

You were a breath ungasped –
an idea I failed to grasp.

You passed up the chance to firm your bones:
to become our own fourth cornerstone;
and yes, made alchemy, fused and split –
did we appal you so? Could that be it?

I shouldn't grieve, you'd barely started –
it's sentimental to be broken-hearted.

It's not as though we'd never met:
I'd hardly dreamed your nature yet,

but how is it you changed your mind
after the promise of a strong blue line?

You couldn't face the wakeful nights?
Not want your part in daily fights?

Chose not to join our shouts and harsh affray;
chose, after all, to stay away

from all I'd offer in such soft redress?
This *No* in answer to my *Yes.*

SEPARATION

I left, *I* packed the bag:
Took off the ring.
Surely I should not cry
But sing.

But this is a strange land
Of empty freedoms;
Empty hands:
Loss and time.

It's not regret I feel
But I'm a refugee:
Sad to lose what Home
Was meant to be.

WASHED UP

At the edge of England
my children stray
on coarse grey beaches;
tug their father
through lacklustre waves.

With you the sea was different:
translucent to the sand,
shot with light,
and opal trumpet fish
dissolved on sight.

There, just beyond
the shade of palms,
we soaked our skin
in sun and arms,
like making love in glass.

L'ABONDANZA

My arm is long from holding hands
With nymphs beside me, skipping;
And though these children play me hard
My lips are soft from kissing.

My eyes are drawn with pencil lines,
My chiffon dress complete.
He even gave me jewellery
And sandals for my feet.

But round my head my curls give way
To shapeless, nameless doubt.
I see the shadow of another child;
An arm that's been rubbed out.

Deborah Mason

MISSING IN ACTION 1917

It was a day of dry hands catching on silk;
of static shocks. The wind breathed in and out,
wheezing and whistling, preparing to blow.
She was smoothing cream into chapped hands
when the telegram came. The door-knob crackled.
Hair frizzed round her face. She read silently,
on an intake of breath. Said nothing. The boy turned
and walked down the path. She watched him go.
Tried to breathe. In and out. Tried not to tremble.

Nancy Mattson

STASH

I hide them away in a tin box
with a hinge, a sailor on the lid
I read them all again and again
in order, backward, sometimes

shuffle them or shut my eyes
pick a single leaf at random
like a raffle ticket from a basket
to catch myself by surprise

Remember the cat we had
that pounced at its own shadow
on the wall or dust in the light
for lack of a fresh mouse?

Your letters never become stale
but I handle them so much

my fingers can read them
their words are in my bones

their paper scarified along the folds
air threaded between words
I know so well I recite them
as I scrub sheets on the washboard

rub my knuckles against its ribs
wishes against facts, your words

as intimate as clothes
softened by years of washing
as tough as sinews
holding my body tight

Tony Maude

THE COMMITTAL

Huddled like vultures gathered round a corpse,
dressed in white shirts, black ties, dark suits, black shoes,
they take their cues from those who are more used
to such solemn meetings. They take the cords
into reluctant hands and pull them tight,
and lift the load away from wooden props
(efficiently removed), lower the box,
then loose the ropes and bow their heads; such light
work for these heavy-hearted men who grieve
the passing of their sister, mother, wife;
each now alone with memories of her life,
not hearing words of faith they don't believe.
With *Amen* said to Father, Spirit, Son
the congregation leaves, their duty done.

Anna Meryt

THE HOSPICE

Strange to be in a place
where death walks
in every corridor
in every room.

I am oppressed by its silent presence
by the heavy scent of flowers
by the silent weeping relatives
in the corners of the lounge,
by the low murmuring voices.

Each day a new set of faces
a new occupant in the bed
then another and then another,
the slow procession of the dead
black and quiet.

And when I come out
the small energy left in me
wants to talk loud,
dance and sing,

to show that I am alive.

HEROES AND GHOSTS
WISH YOU WERE HERE....

When I sleep, your ghost
sleeps beside me.
Your ghost sits in that kitchen chair,
smoking and talking
watching me cook, clean.

Today in the shop
I had to back away
from the men's clothes
to avoid your ghost
in every aisle.

And yesterday,
on a morning walk to the park
your ghost flitted through the shadows
of that copse of young trees
taking photos of me
in the snow.

I want to shout:
come back, come back, come back.
but I don't....

Your ghost scoops up the cat
with big brown hands
and strokes her gently.
In your absence
she has retreated
further into sleep

I wish I could do the same.

Joan Michelson

WIFE

I thought that you had died. Were dead.
So I set off to find a house
for just us two, your wife and child.

I reached a village built on rock
that faced a surging wind-swept sea
and climbed past jumble to the top,

and found you there alive and flush
opening a door for me.
Come in, you said, *Come meet my love.*

You led me up a spiral stair
inside a tower made of stone
with slits for light. And it grew dark,

too dark to see your other wife.
But I could hear and feel her breathe.
And so, I said, *you've a new life.*

Then I was taken with the thought
that you had found the place we sought
when you and I shared dreams and talked.

But you – and this I should have known –
the soul that wanders finds a home,
wordless, returned me to the road.

SLEEP

We were young. No one bothered
much with clothes. You tried a few
other girls before we met
but none passed the test you set.
What mattered was how you slept.

With me, you professed to rest.
So the marriage we grew into,
which failed so many other tests
and tested us until the last,
lasted until death.

And now undressed and wrapped in sheets,
I move from bed to bed to couch
as if reproached by sleep itself.
I lie awake and watch the dark.
I watch a thousand things unseen.

And when the cat returns at dawn
and he curls up, I think of us
as once we slept. Then I could rest.

John Miles

GIRL ON THE SEAFRONT

She stays there all day, eyes turned to the sea.
Oh, when will my darlin' come back 'ome to me?
'e's a-sailin' to Spain, or p'raps round the 'orn.
My life is so empty now 'arry 'as gone.

'E's seeking 'is fortune the best way 'e can,
it's lonely, this love for a sea-farin' man,
but we're plighted together, faithful and true
an' we're to be wed when the next trip is through.

The lads from the village, they wink as I pass,
an' the Squire's son says I'm a fine buxom lass.
There's chartered accountants and fisher-folk 'ere,
but none is as artful as 'arry, my dear.

So I'm true to 'is memory, despite what they say,
and sewin' and savin' and wastin' away.
For when 'e returns 'e will make me 'is own,
and I'll spend my life with my sailor at home.

Well, 'e's back, from the oilfields, with cash in five figures
and I'm sick of crude stories of North Sea oil-riggers.
'E's oily for breakfast, and late for 'is tea,
there's more grease in my washtub than under the sea.

She works on all day, eyes turned to the land,
the beach-tar has covered what's left of the sand.
With the child and the baking, the launderette sack,
her life is too full now that Harry's come back.

Elma Mitchell

TURNING OUT THE MATTRESSES

When we were turning out the mattresses,
Fooling and laughing and heaving and calling across,
I suddenly remembered: you aren't here.
And stood, shaken to pieces by the loss;
As we were turning out the mattresses,
I had to go on. Irreparable distresses,
Eloquent elegies, the waste of tears
Aren't for women with supper to get and all.
It was only a year ago, the funeral
To the time of turning out the mattresses.

This bit of paper's your memorial.

Andrew Motion

THE MOWER

With storm light in the east but no rain yet
I came in from mowing my square of lawn
and paused in the doorway to glance round
at my handiwork and the feckless apple blossom

blurring those trim stripes and Hovver-sweeps
I had meant to last. What I saw instead was you
in threadbare cords, catching the sunny interval
between showers, trundling the Ransome out

From its corner in the woodshed. The dizzy whiff
of elm chips and oil. Joke-shop spider threads
greying the rubber handles. Gravel pips squeaking
as the roller squashed through the yard. Then a hush

like the pause before thunder while you performed
your ritual of muffled curses and fore-head wipes,
your pessimistic tugs on the starter cable,
more curses, more furious yanks, until at long last

the engine sulked, recovered, sighed a grey cloud
speckled with petrol-bits, and wobbled into a roar.
Off came the brake and off charged the machine,
dragging you down to the blazing Tree of Heaven

at the garden end, where the trick was to reverse
without stalling or scraping a hefty mud-crescent,
before you careered back towards Kit and me
at our place in the kitchen window, out of your way.

To and fro, to and fro, to and fro, to and fro,
and each time a few feet more to the left, sometimes
lifting one hand in a hasty wave which said *Stay put!*
but also *I'm in charge!,* although we understood

from the way your whole body lurched lopsided
on the turn, this was less than a hundred percent true.
Getting the job done was all we ever wanted,
parked with our cricket things and happy enough

to wait, since experience had taught us that after
you'd unhooked the big green metal grass-basket
with its peeling *By Royal Appointment* transfer,
lugged it off to the smoking heap by the compost,

thumped it empty, then re-appeared to give us
the thumbs up, we were allowed to burst suddenly
out like dogs into the sweet air, measure the pitch
between our studious stump-plantings, toss to see

who went in first, then wait for you to turn up again
from the woodshed where you had taken five minutes
to switch the petrol off, and wipe the blades down,
and polish the grass-basket although it never would

shine up much, being what you called venerable.
You always did come back, that was the thing.
As you also come back now in the week you died,
just missing the first thick gusts of rain and the last

of the giddy apple blossom falling into your footprints,
with bright grass-flecks on your shoes and trouser-legs
carefree for the minute, and young, and fit for life,
but cutting clean through me then vanishing for good.

SERENADE

There were the two ponies –
and there was Serenade, which belonged
to my mother. Though 'who belonged'
would be better, in view of the girlish head-lift

she had, and her flounce to and fro in the lumpy field
and that big womanish rump I always gave a wide berth to.
When the blacksmith came to shoe her, which was seldom
in summer, but otherwise often, she would let him hoist

and stretch out first one hind leg, then the other,
with a definitely melancholy, embarrassed restraint.
The blacksmith was ferret-faced and rat-bodied,
hardly man enough to keep aloft the great weight

of one-foot-at-a-time, though he did keep it sort of
aloft, crouched over double, and bent at the knees,
to make a peculiar angle which held each hoof still
on his battle-scarred apron. He would set up shop

under the covered entrance-way between
our house and the stable block: a ramshackle
clapboard affair, black (or black weathering to green),
with swallows' mud villages proliferating in the rafters.

I liked it there in the drive-through,
which was also where we parked the car (but not
on his days) – for the oil-maps on the dusty cement
brilliant as the wet skin of a trout, and for the puzzling

swallow-shit patterns, and most of all for that place
by the corner drain where a grass-snake had appeared
once, an electric-green, sleepy-looking marvel
which, when it disappeared, left a print of itself

that stayed in the mind for ever. The blacksmith
always did cold shoeing, prising off each thin moon-
crescent, then carving the hoof with a bone-handled,
long-bladed knife. The miracle of no pain!

Serenade gone loose in her skin, her strength
out of her, so she seemed suspended in water,
her hypnotised breathing steady, the smell of piss
and musty hay and ammonia sweat coming off her,

her head dropping down, eyes half-closed now,
and me a boy watching the earth-stained sole of her hoof
turning pure white as the blacksmith pared and trimmed,
leaving the nervous diamond of the frog well alone

but showing me, just by looking, how even to touch that,
much worse cut it, would wake her and break the spell
and our two heads with it. Our collie dog sat near
where the snake had been, ravenous black and white,

all ears, sometimes fidgeting her two slim front feet,
glancing away as if about to dash off, then twisting back,

licking her lips and swallowing with a half-whine.
She knew better than to get under anyone's feet,

but when the blacksmith had done with his cutting,
and offered a new shoe, and fiddled it downwards
or sideways, and hammered it with quick hits
which drove the nail-points clean through (but these

could be filed off later, and were) – when this was all
done, he kicked the clippings across the cement
and now it was the collie's turn to show a sad restraint,
taking one delicate piece between her pink lips, ashamed

to be a slave of appetite, and curving away into the yard
to eat it in private. The blacksmith straightened himself,
one hand smoothing the small of his back, the other picking
a few remaining nails from his own darker lips,

then slapped Serenade on the flank with his red palm,
rousing her from her trance, running his fingers up
her mane and all over her ears, giving each a soft tug
and saying *She'll do,* or *Good lady,* or *There's a girl.*

Whereupon my mother herself appeared to pay him –
their hands met, and touched, and parted,
and something passed between them – and the blacksmith
took off his apron, with its colours of a battered tin bowl,

folded it, and carried it before him in a lordly fashion,
using it as a cushion for his collapsed bag of hammers,
clippers, knives, files, pliers and nails to the van
which he had parked in the lane some distance from us

while my mother untied the halter and led her horse away.
There was a crisp clip-clop over the stable yard,
and a train of hoof-prints with the neat shoes obvious to me,
who had stayed behind with nothing better to do than look.

This was Serenade, who would later throw my mother
as they jumped out of a wood into sunlight, and who,
taking all possible pains not to trample her down, or even
touch her, was nevertheless the means to an end, which

was death. Now I am old as my mother was then,
at the time of her fall, and I can see Serenade clearly
in her own later life, poor dumb creature nobody blamed,
or could easily like any more either, which meant nobody

came to talk to her much in the spot she eventually found
under the spiky may tree in the field, and still less
came to shoe her, so her hooves grew long and crinkled
round the edges like wet cardboard (except they were hard)

while she just stood there not knowing what she had done,
or went off with her girlish flounce and conker-coloured arse,
waiting for something important to happen, only nothing ever did,
beyond the next day and the next, and one thing leading to another.

Beryl Myers

ALONE

Hum-drum, humming to herself,
busy, she flicks her duster,
along the shelf, over the picture of a child,
now grown and flown the nest.

Flustered she finds
memories flickering through her mind…
a sunny day, a hand in hers,
the smell of hay, of flowers,

of happy hours gleaned long ago.
No, no…. She must be strong.
Floors to be cleaned, work to be done,
she must go on alone.

She leans against the sink.
The water in the bowl swirls the washing-up.
She thinks of little girls,
curls flying in the wind, gathering buttercups.

She sits mending, fending off her heart's ache.
She sorts the colours in their box.
An iridescent dragonfly darts across the lake…
the devil's darning needle, darning her socks.

Why do such sharp visions prick her eyes,
spinning through her head, giving her no rest?
Why is the past so vibrant and today so dead?

Sylvia Oldroyd

COMING OF AGE

Child whom I know so well, yet never knew,
today each heart-beat echoes back your name.
Though years recede, I keep you still in view,

feeling the weight of empty days, in lieu
of life's experience you could not claim;
child whom I know so well, yet never knew.

This gathering of your namesake rose, I do
once more, to hold remembrance just the same.
Though years recede I keep you still in view;

for comfort, birthday's salving rites renew,
illuminate your night with living flame.
Child whom I know so well, yet never knew,

charged with this ever-present sense of you
the hurt translates to words within a frame;
though years recede, I keep you, still in view.

Between these lines, your essence filters through,
a distant star-shine steadfast in its aim.
Child whom I know so well, yet never knew,
light-years recede; I keep you still, in view.

AFTERSHOCK

It should be geological in scale.
Seismic. And much of the time it is.
The word *never* triggers earth-movements
of cataclysmic proportion.

But now and then I regain balance enough
to move life along, push the day
forward with rituals of routine:
dress, eat, form words, make plans, even jokes,

while walking an egg-shell crust
barely hardened. Because it's always there,
this subterranean intrusion:

persistent gravel in the shoe;
perpetual grit in the eye;
dead-weight of your absence.

WHITE CHRISTMAS

This year an absence
in the window-corner;
absence of green.
No raising of resinous spruce.
Baubles remain wrapped,
collected over lifetimes,
their histories
become poignant.

This year the tree is white.
As wired branches spread
under my fingers, it takes shape;
pure as frosted breath
exhaled in December dawns,
when every blade in the field
was armoured in rime. You were
always a winter man.

Unstarred, the tree astonishes;
such brilliant lack of colour.
I twine pale flower lights
among paper needles,
glitter it with tinsel,
hang a few silver drops
without associations.
When the lights fail
on the third morning
it seems fitting.

This year I keep Christmas
remembering you; your taste
for the sparse, the spare,
the undecorated. This year
the tree is white; the colour
of silence

Vicky Olliver

BIRTHDAY

My father died
two days before his birthday.
My card,
To the best dad in the world,
was sent as absolution,
was never opened,
left things unsaid,
remained unread.
When I last went to kiss him,
he turned away his head.

NOVEMBER, NORTH WALES

Someone stood at the gate smiling.
Someone asked for help with map reading.
Someone carried food on a tray
to a friend who was ill.

Beyond bare trees I saw two wind-turbines
turn on a hilltop,
saw dark clouds cover cottages like smoke.
In the garden I saw embers fly from a morning bonfire.

In my mind's eye I saw my father
fall again in the kitchen,
saw my father fall
again and again.

David Olsen

VERTIGO

Once,
I could venture on to a roof
to replace a broken tile,
clear a downspout of fallen leaves,
or align a skewed antenna;
I could balance and bear the risk.

I could go to the edge with you,
trusting the truth of your belay,
where precipice allowed no return
and we held nothing back.
Once upon a fairy-tale time,
I had no fear of falling.

Jennie Osborne

HAND-ME-DOWNS

Ten years on, I still wear her clothes,
her short blue jacket, her stylish raincoat lined
with her habit of thrift, make do and mend.

As each year ticks away, those few remaining
of her generation tell me how, as I too age,
increasingly I wear her face.

I wear, have always worn, her dash
and scurry, over-eagerness to fetch
and carry, inability to rest,

and every night into the bin I throw
her worry lines, the lines she learnt by heart:
I am not good enough, I am not good enough.

AMBUSH

It has to be November
and I'm ambushed
by Mendelssohn
the violin concerto
old favourite
I skip over these days.

I'm clutching the pine table
find myself staring
at rain pouring from a choked gutter
an old cloth
abandoned in the yard
grey as the day.

I want to rescue it
wring out dirty water
wring out Mendelssohn's notes
and pain in some deep part I can't name

change the music to Pachelbel or Bach
something that believes
in a pattern,
get back to clean and white again.

Katherine T Owen

A SINGLE SENTENCE

I meet an old friend in a department store.
How are you? I ask.
My mother is dying of cancer, she replies.

A single sentence which implies
immeasurable loss and grief,
change of view on self and
of relationships.

A single sentence she repeats
to various reactions
from shock to lack of interest.

Sometimes not telling a friend.
Then telling a complete stranger
because *everyone* should know.
Yet only her own world falls
apart.

And there should be
sad music,
a change of lighting.
Instead there is only
a single sentence.

William Oxley

A CHARM AGAINST LOSS

I would just keep
the country for me
as an old apple
in the grubby pocket of the city,
and from time to time
take it out and see

it had not shrivelled
altogether but was
a still ripe reminder
of what I love because
in streets one needs not food
but charm against the loss

of mist-growth, roots
and sandy sun,
of long still waters
fields where horses run
and wind-mocked leaves
that whisper: *Life is never done.*

THE GIFT OF YOUR WAYS

At the passing by of the days
At the flowing by of the waters of life
I shall remember your ways
That made all the glories of life,
That raised up for me a joy
That is beyond all means of praise.

For I am a man who was once a boy
Who can do no more at the passing of days
At the flowing by of the waters of life
Than remember the gift of your ways,
For which the falling of my thanks
Is as the showering of leaves upon grass,
Is as the whisper of flowers on banks –
A gratitude for a love that cannot pass.

HE WAS MY PROSPERO

He was my Prospero, my guide
and I think him still alive
somewhere in the undergrowth of silence
that surrounds our life, our dreams.

Where the sad, the sick, find menace,
but others gleam of immeasurable hope,
he is my ghost, indwelling impalpable one
that I choose to live on –
tenant of my darkest dark
a spark of imagined light.

Father, who helped me grow,
lost forever to this dramatic earth,
gave me generous birth,
lacked in himself ego
like one too wise for it –
but could hand on love –
which is enough, more than enough.

Jeremy Page

FADING

And I wonder
how long you will know me,
how long until I join
the bit part players,
characters who made
their first appearance
after you had lost the plot.

How long until
the fragile line between me
and everyone else dissolves,
until I might be son or
grandson, casual acquaintance,
best friend or the man
from the gas board.

I know how it ends,
I've read the books –
while you, thank God,
have not

Mark Pasco

THROUGH THE LOOKING-GLASS

I took half her smile out
To rinse.

Words swirled about her
Like a lifetime's leaves

In a lifetime's autumns:
Colours and decay
Flying, falling.

Strawberry pips had winkled their way.

My nearly-ninety
Artist, teacher, gardener,
Twice-widowed mother of five.

I think she mostly knew me,

Shadow-dancing
Her former self
Through dementia's twilight

Between worlds.

I fed, read; showed
Her photographs,
Wrapped her in the love
Of holding hands
And surprised looks.

She was the youngest of five herself,
The baby bird, plumped,
Open-mouthed, vulnerable.

Wandering hums
Nomadic meanings
Bright ribbons of memory
Drifted between us.

Mourning my mother
Would sigh
Along the homeward road.

For this rare moment
The venerable patchwork
Of her rich, full, cherished life
Spread between us.

A soft and long embrace,
Farewell. Her smell.
Her question, *So –*
How are your parents?

Robert Peake

THE SILENCE TEACHER

Seeing friends for the first time after his death
tested the silence a room could hold. The rest
was a kindness like holding our breath.

My wife's oldest friend offers her best
brave smile, tells us about the first time
her daughter, in new hearing aids, passed a nest.

Pitched as high as a tin wind chime,
in a sphere beyond the rumble of speech
she only knew *tweet* from what mother had mimed.

But birds' hunger songs seemed as far from reach
as the angels Blake saw perched in a tree,
and sweeter than any science her mother could teach.

Her world was based partly on what she could see.
The rest was a guess – the flailing of a street preacher
seemed like the swats of a man attacked by bees.

Quick lips make it easy to misread a speaker,
and once at a party, based on what she had seen,
the girl introduced her mother as a *silence teacher*.

Grief's small hands cupped before me,
reliving the news of our infant son's tests,
his brain as quiet as her soundless sea,

and still as winter in a robin's nest,
I did not say: *I was the one who held him last
until the ticking heart stopped in his chest*

or what that silence taught, and how it pressed.

Pat Perry

STONE

I am as a stone
buried in black earth
blindly burrowing
downward.

I am as the earth itself
black grains
filling the hollow
the stone displaces.

I am as the closed sound
of the falling earth:
dumbly seeking
its own level.

The stone is enclosed
by its own blind eye,
is deaf to the earth's
resounding silence;

both are alone.

Yet the black earth
hugs to the stone
in rain,

in a dry time
rains loud on the
hollow coffin.

Now is a season of narrow rain
and shut horizons.

A FINE AND PRIVATE PLACE

Your limp anemones lie beside him now
as you once did, soft on the silky bib and tucker,
dark eyes closed on their pain.
Soon another lid will close
sealing in forever that ultimate sad deception.
Even in death you could not claim him,
your name can never share his epitaph
as you once shared his bed.
In church you stand alone,
small with grief; coiffured
chrysanthemums curl crisply on the coffin.
His wife and family standing stiffly, can't forgive
the fact he's left them twice –
though this time's more respectable.

Jo Peters

MY GRANDMOTHER'S HOUSE

today I butter a slice of toast
push my knife in
right through the hard crust
bring it out clean then
dip it into marmalade
and I'm eight again
in a sunny room where breakfast's set
I'm watching her knife do just that
basking in not being one of four
somehow knowing she was my treat
I was hers

I smell the lemon verbena's warm scent
see faded watercolours
of Egypt   Greece   sense the hint
of foreignness   adventure
taste an exotic treat
long spaghetti with grated cheese
feel our complicity
in the grown-up thrill of being up late
slapping cards down for Racing Demon
a safe rivalry salted by
the knowledge she too wanted to win

oh – and her hair was waist length
wound in a soft coil deftly pinned
the same colour as mine
greying black
what unconsidered thing that I do now
will one day bring me back?

Mario Petrucci

IF YOU WERE TO COME BACK

I'd stand at the door like one bereaved:
Aghast and breathless,
With silence stretched between us
For a second
Before it snapped –
And my heart burst its banks
In belief.

Then I'd draw you in by both hands
I'd kiss you on the mouth, on the face
Wear out your name
              with soft saying
I'd kiss you more than you would want
Until you'd have to draw back, breathless
As one wounded
To try to speak, to tell me
Why it was you came.

THE ROOM
(Chernobyl, 1986)

This hospital has a room

for weeping. It has no crèche.
No canteen. No washroom queue.

Only this queue for weeping.
No lost property booth. No

complaints department. Or
reception. No office of second

opinion. Of second chances. Its sons
and daughters die with surprise

in their faces. But mothers
must not cry before them. There is

a room for weeping. How hard
the staff are trying. Sometimes

they use the room themselves. They
must hose it out each evening.

The State is watching. They made
this room for weeping. No remission –

no quick fixes. A father wonders
if his boy is sleeping. A mother

rakes her soul for healing. Neighbours
in the corridor – one is screaming

It moved from your child to mine.
More come. Until the linoleum

blurs with tears and the walls
are heaving. Until the place can't

catch its breath – sour breath
of pine. And at its heart

this room.

ARK

With you here, I had a zoological time.
At the sink I slobbered your nape

with bloodhound kisses, paw on each shoulder.
Was all meerkat for your key in the door.

In the shower I'd be robin, cheeping
my heart out from a steam-basted chest.

Under dawn duvets I was squirrel-whiskered –
fossicked and dug you, all scratchy-toed.

Cold evenings, iguana, I'd slow-lick
lips, all-foured around your trunk.

And when you said I was your man
I brayed so they heard it in Bosotoland.

Now you're gone, they cower under lock and key.
Come back. Bring out the animals in me.

STROKE

You're a perfect likeness of yourself. But that
clot knotted your brain, a dark fertilisation.

And though you blinked and breathed where you lay face-
up on the kitchen floor – your beige enamel bowl of eggs

overturned on the tiles – even though you looked at us
and blinked, you were gone. Four minutes without

oxygen. All it takes to discharge a lifetime.

I dream that beige bowl. Watch it surface through the tiles
upturned – like some mother-god of chaos, crazed

and chapped, simply unbroken, acolytes splashed in its wake.
In daylight now you shuffle, chew. Sometimes even hum

a few notes – wind-chimes in the blank doorway of your head.
Drift around the house rehearsing the one track. Flesh ghost.

Perhaps, somewhere, your yolk's intact. Breakfast, we watch you
crash the top off a soft-boiled. Natalia points –

That's the way she did it, when she was alive.

LAST WORDS

What were they? you ask.
What? What did he say
exactly?

Truth is, I couldn't hear.
Though I leaned so far
the blood

in his breath made me gag.
I'll settle for that
silver beach

forty years back – his gift
of gritty ice-cream. Hand
like a socket

to the ball of my shoulder.
The way he leaned
so close

I thought his breathing
the sea. *Good boy*
he told me.

Ellen Phethean

ROWING HOME

Tears are the ocean,
pain is his boat –
he'll cross with the oars
of love into the blunt dark,
leaving all light behind.

Let him go.

AN ANCIENT CALLING

Consulting clocks, they come with quiet tread
to rooms that echo, lit up day and night,
where unsuspecting people, agitated,
face men in black with questioning looks, or white
crisp women bearing basin, flannel, soap.
They know procedure if we're blank
or lost, they're kindly when we're stunned, all hope
forgone. They lead us to that river bank
where we must hear of who's to cross and why.
Appointed from above, they understand
our wilderness, and even as we cry,
regardless, move us on. We hold their hand
and love them. We would follow them to hell,
they deliver agony so well.

VOW

(after Carol Ann Duffy)

At the back of a drawer
you have scattered the stars;
I hide long lists.

Time slips and drifts,
dawn snags with blue cries.
I turn like the seasons

through endless space
with no country to sail to
where you are.

If I was dead
I'd take your hand
from the huge northern sky
face the sun
get up, get out of bed.

Nicky Phillips

TRAPPED

Some days I indulge myself,
picture you free, hear again
our youthful screams of delight
on a merry-go-round, relive
holidays with scampering children,
wet tarpaulins on Cornish beaches,
imagine your proud smile over
a blue-flamed Christmas pudding.

Then I look at your face and see
love, memory, knowledge all trapped
inside your brain, no longer knowing how
to liberate, use nor extend themselves.
Behind your eyes, our past,
imprisoned, marinating.
Our present too, confused.
And our future? Who knows?

Just sometimes, the old you flits back,
a flicker of recognition, as scudding clouds
reveal, for an instant, a full moon.
Something leaps, my pulse quickens
but fast, too fast, shutters are drawn back
down by your puzzled expression
and we are, once more, locked apart,
your freedom re-stolen.

Dorothy Pope

NOT YET

Unread and daily set aside
to be recycled,
his copy of *The Times* arrives
and I
can no more bear
to cancel it
than I can part
with his good overcoat
or give away
his favourite marmalade.

Sue Proffitt

TWO SISTERS

are dying

The one who loves her garden must go North.
It is dark, too cold for her fingers in the earth.
Splinters cut her hands, scraping the soil's hard edge.
In the black rocks there are seams of green
but the sun's lemonade-wedge light is short;
she must pull herself in at dusk.

The one who hates her garden must go West
where the earth turns all night under a gold sky.
There is no sunrise here in this fallow silence,
just the stirring of sleepless worms
where she keeps company with other kneelers,
hands rising and falling like sickles over the soil.

That's how it is.

IN THE SADNESS OF SPRING

In the sadness of Spring
my mother chews
the gravelly bread of memory,
hunting meaning's nub, retreating
to the comfort-cud of repetition.

In the sadness of Spring
in the luminous dusk
she grasps for thought-holds
that crumble — flails
in the terrored space —

catches a child's words, pulls
on the lifeline of my still-remembered love.

As she folds the clipped wings
of her cardigan round her,
sits, shifts,   recoils
from the bright insistent grab of questions
without answers,
I see her face change –

pulling the hood over her eyes,
her features sharpen.
Something older peers out
from the bony-shouldered dark –
beaked, benignly empty,
appraising the land
that's gone to waste.

Jay Ramsay

YEARS ON, YEARS LATER, AND
(i.m. C.E.D.)

Forgiveness was your face raised in the sun
a momentary encounter we couldn't have planned
after all that, it was as easy as laughing.

She says you must be retired now.
It all fades into the same eternal summer
now the years tilt in the direction of death –

like this glinting light: like a golden bowl
full of liquid sunlight.

I think of you gone ahead finding out

where she is, in the same flute-played light
you had to tell me she'd died in…

walking towards me across a telescopic distance

we finally bridged in seconds.

Jeremy Robson

NO ANSWER
(for my mother, Charlotte)

It snowed the week you died.
An early spring blessing
some would say,
but I'd rather there'd been sun
to warm you on your way.

Earlier there was mud,
everywhere, then rain,
shovels at half tilt. Is this
a joke you've played on us?
Can we begin again?

There's no answer
from the telephone
no-one at the door.
However hard we call
we'll hear from you no more.

Ghosts and echoes fill the empty flat,
here the armchair where you always sat,
there the floppy hat you sometimes wore,
and in the dusty dressing-table drawer,
the fading pearls you kept for best.

It's cold, a window has been left ajar
and the evening breeze is snatching
at the curtain nets, petals spatter
the carpeted floor. Once full of song
this place is now an empty stage.
The piano waits, but the star has gone.

Mark Roper

SILENCE

In your room you sit
with Silence.

Just a few small things
beside you.

She's asked you to clear
some space for her.

She doesn't leave now
when we come in.

When we talk
she tries to interrupt.

You keep looking
across at her.

We can almost
see her too.

We too begin to fall
under her spell.

Soon she insists
we leave.

She wants you
all to herself.

LAST BREATH

Though you couldn't swallow,
had taken no food for weeks,
your breathing wouldn't stop.

In and out, slow and steady
as the stroke of an oar,
it just kept on going.

As if that breathing
had become a pair of oars,
rowing of their own accord.

Each stroke rowing you
further away from us,
deeper into the distance

until, with the slightest click,
those oars were docked.

PUBLIC

After they had removed your body
and after Ann had tidied the house,
one room was still full of metal and rubber,
all the scaffolding needed to keep you up,
cushions, hoist, frames, wheelchair,

bath-lift, special bed, alarm.
Props waiting for another stage.

It had been such a show. So public.
And you were such a private soul.
You who hated the show of any feeling.
As soon as they began to treat you,
as soon as you were touched, you withdrew.
You'd never have said, but it's there in photos,
that set of mouth, that puzzle in your eyes.

Like a bird whose broken wing heals
in captivity, but which won't even try
to fly again, you lost the will to live.
All that weakness on show, you grew
more and more helpless. Unbearable,
never to be really on your own.

Unable to find a quiet corner to die,
you hid, in the only place you could,
inside yourself. You left your face behind,
crawled away deeper and deeper.
It took you a long time to manage.
But you got there in the end.

Michael Rosen

UNTITLED

thank you for your card. I can't answer your
question: *What can I say?* as I don't know what
to say either. You're right, it is a loss. It reminds
me that I lost him. He was there. Then he
wasn't. Though in between, he was blue and

stiff and landed with a thud when 999 told
me to pull him to the floor. Yes, it is unfair and
cruel. It also makes me tired with a
tiredness that hangs on like a dog. It's nice of
you to say you'll always remember him. You won't.

Diana Sanders

DARKNESS

The rook looks,
peering from old eyes
that shine from the shadow side.

He sees how the light turns
and how the ivy gathers
and how the page has crumbled
and how the words are scattered.

He beats time on the roof.
Tap, tap.
Tap, tap.

The clock stops.

Geoff Sanderson

ST MICHAELS

It almost seemed as if someone had given her a happy pill!
The cancer, widely embedded in her brain, had switched
off the 'worry' part first. From diagnosis to death six weeks

later, she was happy and untroubled. Her family came to
say their last good-byes, then she slipped away one evening
– dying as she had lived, quietly, peacefully, and with dignity.

A loud knock at the door heralded the ambulance men:
noisy, cheerful, brisk, they wrapped you up and skilfully
moved you into the ambulance.

***

As we entered the gates, the Hospice wrapped its arms
around us, gave us a welcoming hug. The door closed
behind us, and the peace, the goodness of the place
descended on us.

***

The next day – wonder of wonders – I found you sitting up
in your chair, sheets of newspaper scattered at your feet.
You told me about the excellent food, the kindness of the staff,
how happy you felt.

***

And so it went, day after day, as you slowly sank toward the place
where I couldn't follow. One day, your eyelids flickered open,
your fingers raised from the bed in a feeble gesture:
Hello, I see you there, they said.

***

The phone call came at 9pm. I hurriedly got ready,
drove to the Hospice, heart beating wildly.
The nurse's kindly face told me all I needed to know.
I sat with you, stroked your arm, gave you a final kiss,
then tiptoed from the room.

POSTSCRIPT — HAIKU

returning to
the empty house...
thoughts echo

hall stand...
her walking stick
now unused

breakfast cereal...
I still reach for
two spoons

her magazine
in its plastic wrapper...
Sunday morning

Roses
and yet more roses...
her legacy.

Jane Saunders

NEW YEAR

each moment of joy
and excitement
is accompanied at the edges
by that small package
of loss.

a dog scampers across the
crisp blue day
as the sun hangs low
like a frosted orange, spreading shadows

deep in the brightness of the present,
the past calls out its memories.
Time runs along beside me.

EDGES

death is just a breath away
from the clutter and mess of living
yet still we avert our gaze
to fix on a distant horizon
and risk losing the ground we inhabit
forgetting this moment is all

Linda Saunders

KEEPING THE FIRE

When mother was very old I'd cup both
her hands in mine and blow on them
to encourage the spark. We kept her life in
like the fire in the grate, damped down
to the utmost, close as a forbidden faith.
When it went out, her spirit clung to my hair
with a smell of smoke; it was so cold my grief
froze even before it could leave my eyes.

Later I went to the church with my dark
lanthorn to beg a flame again. Finding the way
by starlight, I heard the hiss of the frost
like the stars breathing, and was possessed
by the sense of lives countless as the stars,
each mind a candle lit from the one source.
At the helm of my vision I shielded
such knowledge against the wind of reason.

Seven wells of tallow in the Cresset Stone
light the days in turn as they circle
the central flame that must never fail.
I held my taper to the hallowed fire
then turned down my wick till it burned blue
as her eyes were beneath a yellow crown.
now I shall rekindle my hearth and throw
on fir cones for the hot smell of resin.

Myra Schneider

LOSING
(for Stephen)

Every sock in the bunch you're holding
is a dangling single. You wonder how many more
must be mouldering, partnerless, stuck in drawers.

Later, on the way to work, you remember
the lost mug patterned with rosemary you think
an absent-minded friend slipped into her bag,

and picture the half-dead umbrella you left on a bus.
But all this is trivial on a day when the smudged air
is buzzing with the loss of jobs, self-respect, children.

Hopeless, you fold the newspaper, turn to now –
this moment on a train underground: that black lad,
beautiful in his pale blue anorak. You try to work out

why his hands are across his eyes. To block out
the world as he listens to the sound wires
are bringing to his ears? To survey the carriage?

Already this now has passed out of reach, become
a memory which will sink or swim among millions
of others in your mind's measureless caverns.

And now, you visualise time as unstoppable sand falling
through a sieve, count the growing refusals
of your body. They remind you a moment will come

when you'll lose the privilege of consciousness,
remind you not to hang around limply as a sock
but to forestall this last loss with findings:

a sparrowhawk perched on your gate, eyes alert
for prey, words that toadleap from imagination,
from heart – to make sure every day is a finding.

STILLNESS

In darkness let your fan of fingers open,
imagine amethyst's purple crystals
at a geode's heart liquefying to honey
until your face muscles loosen, your shoulders,
which have borne so much, begin to unlock
and stillness is a quilt over your body,
a feather lining within. Now the tock
of pulse emerges and breath passes quietly
as a slippered friend. Beyond the house tyres
whirr on tarmac and geese call as they rush
the sky. The grief of the bereaved will push
into your room and nameless losses sustained
by the displaced. Hold stillness and you may hear
rain on fruitless fields, grasses rising again.

TODAY THERE IS TIME

to touch the silken stillness
of myself, map its landscape,
the missing left breast, to lay
my nervous palm softly
as a bird's wing across
the new plain, allow
tears to fall yet rejoice
the surgeon has scraped
away the cancer cells.

Today there is time
to contemplate the way life
opens, clams, parts, savour
its remembered rosemaries,
spreading purples, tight
white edges of hope, to travel
the meanings of repair, tug
words that open parachutes.

Lynne Sedgemore

SLIPPING AWAY

You slipped away unseen
like a shadow in the night –
such unexpected haste.

Shocked and locked in grief
I live in the shadows now,
barely alive,

grieving and raging and waiting
to fade and slip away
to be with you again.

Jill Sharp

VOYAGE

I lie on the narrow bed, you in my arms.
This is our last night, love, but you are tired.
My mind drifts to another time, your eyes
sea-blue above the old steel-string guitar
we used to sing to; then to your hands'
first rippling touch, my 'wild surmise'!
How we lay coiled upon a single bed
or cavorted across its sturdy frame
like sailors running the spinnaker.
Now we rest, becalmed in the slow swell
of your heaving chest. Beneath the instruments
that chart your path, we sleep. I dream of you
holding me in our little craft, and wake
when your arm falls from me, knowing you've gone.

VALEDICTION

As the black cars glide down the hill
why are you at my shoulder, laughing?
And I can't help smiling to be here
in this flash limousine, a pale bride
in her solemn, slow parade, as you mock
these faces 'playing at funerals.'
Back home, all the glum faces gone, the kids,
expressionless, watch TV. In our room,
dumbfounded, I stroke your plastic lighter
into life, over and over, outstaring
each frail flame. A faceless ghost, the pillow
still holds your head's form; now I rest my own
in that selfsame space, trying to make sense
of a different pronoun and a different tense.

Lindsey Shaw-Miller

CULPA

Drawn lines at your eye,
hold me still;
a bitter, terminal look,
your heart harvest; goodbye.

My own translation
turned my head,
and for that moment's
actless recognition

you give no quarter.
Not I but
you changed your plans,
halted your step for good.

Did I not love you
enough, my
father, could not tell,
could not know that you were

my deepest blue, my
elsewhere friend,
my boredom, my flower,
my precious stone. My grief
without end.

Penelope Shuttle

1. This year no one will ask how you voted,
   or if you know the way to town

   No one will call you as an eye-witness
   or teach you how to train a bird of prey

   No one will bring you your *New Scientist*,
   try to sell you double-glazing
   or tell you their secrets

   People will write to you
   but you won't answer their letters

   The high sheriff of mistletoe
   will never catch our eye again

   No one will peel apples for you,
   or love you more than you can bear

   No one will forget you

2. I wept in Tesco,
   Sainsbury's
   and in Boots

   where they gave me
   medicine for grief

   But I wept in Asda,
   in Woolworths
   and in the library

where they gave me
books on grief

I wept in Clarks
looking in vain for shoes
that would stop me weeping

I wept on the peace march
and all through the war

I wept in Superdrug
where they gave me
a free box of tissues

I wept in the churches,
the empty empty churches,

and in the House of Commons –
they voted me out of office

3. I can't cry anyone's tears except my own,
    can't teach anything but my own ignorance

    I can only fall from my own mountain,
    ledge by ledge

    I can't rival the wasp's sting
    or sew except with my needle

    Like a saltwater wife,
    I prise open the oyster of my loss,

    hoick out the pearl of your death

9. Don't bring me the sea,
    or clouds, or those packs of trees,
    don't bring me night, or stars
    or forthright moons, or the solitude
    of the river; take away
    that farmyard of cyclamen,
    your flooded side-street, don't bring me
    the sun, leave it where it is,
    don't offer me operas or banknotes,
    spider-webs peppered with dew –
    I don't want a bullfight
    or a cushion you've worked yourself –
    I don't want anything except the past,
    bring me five years ago, last winter,
    the week before last, yesterday

10. I make my home in your absence,
    take your smallest hope

    and make it grow

    I wake to the dusk of everywhere
    as if assisting at my own birth

    or arriving in a country
    where all the rivers settle down to be ice

17. Your name didn't change
    after your death –
    many others also answered to it

    After your death
    the climate didn't change,
    the government stayed calm

Waterfalls
remembered you for ever,
remaining loyal,
looking for you everywhere,
storm after storm, teacup after teacup

21. I've lived with your death for a year,
    that despot death, that realist,

    stunned,
    as if I've just given birth to a foal,
    or made an enemy of the rain

    All at once
    you had more important things to do
    than to live

    Death is the feather in your cap,
    the source of your fame,
    my darkest lesson

    This dropout year closes,
    I begin my second year without you,
    just me and the paper-thin world

OVER MY SHOULDER

I look over my shoulder
there you are
after all these years
moving slowly
out of the world
taking your time
like days lost at sea

the silvery snappy sea
the salty sea
our eyes don't meet
that's not what you do
you're holding up
the shield of your life
against all remaining perils
reflecting back every gleam
from your life
to mine
like a small lovely morning
only you and I can see
and now it's gone

MY FATHER'S RESTING PLACE

I bring thoughts and afterthoughts
light of all the skies
too much ocean for any jack-tar
his ship holed in his breast
I bring both forks
of my tongue
my wheeling and pacing mind
to this quiet rainy graveyard
near Ascot
where the retired racing horses
from the neighbouring paddock
lean their long smooth brown muzzles over
munching the flowers we leave for Dad
till we learn our lesson
and bring silk flowers instead
In your wonky heart-of-hearts
(Dad)
you were always tearing up and down
the football pitch or potting shots

across the baize
On the phone your voice was strong
people thought you were a young man
your soul was strong
an all-the-way-to-hell-and-back soul
and here you are
with the browsing horses
the skies the rains the planets the stars
I bring my thoughts but
(Dad)
I'm like a star tired of shining
terrified of the quick-wit telescopes playing over
my surface
seeing the emptiness
so little reason to linger

But I linger here
at my father's resting place

Pat Simmons

UNTIL
(i.m. Hugh)

I am keeping this room swept
until you come back.

I am keeping the bills paid
until you come back.

I am keeping the boiler insured and annually inspected,
my under-arms clean,
the dog vaccinated,
the garden dug

and appropriately planted,
until you come back.

Until you come back
I am singing in your choir,
making sure they remember you,
keeping your seat warm.
I'll teach you the new words
when you come back.

Until you come back
I am keeping my mind
stitched together
with hedgehog spines;
holding my bones
with iron breath
in a roughly skeleton shape;
my blood moving in the right directions
Monday to Tuesday to Wednesday.

But what will you wear
when you come back?
I have given your trousers away
to the Oxfam shop, and your socks
for recycling.

Until you come back
I have scattered your ash
out from the hill
to the lake
and under the trees
of our love.

And when you come back
strolling up from the car park
slowly and in an ordinary sort of way,
stuffing, perhaps, your keys in your pocket

or zipping your jacket up against the cold,
you'll find everything clean,
all in order,
your ashes lying tidy on the wind.

You'll find I've kept faith.

MAPS
(for Hugh)

You have taught me to know
my right hand from my left,
taught me there is a map,
though it floats on chaos
and curls and unfurls
in the sulphurous wind.
You have shown me the arrow
that says, *You are here, now.*
You are you.

This is north, you said, *this south.*
This line is the road from over here to there.
You turn left at that roundabout
for far away,
where we saw the white house
with the green door.

You're safe to go
wherever you want.
Just keep your eyes open,
look all around,
and place one foot
after the other.

I know the earth shifts, you said,

like lemon jelly;
that the sky flips and bucks,
the sea turns itself inside out;
that tomorrow collides
with a week last Monday
and the seventh century B.C.

But north is still north.
You know now where you are.
Go where you choose.
You're safe, you know,
as long as you know
your map co-ordinates
and how to read contours.

Sick and weakened, today
you have stayed behind
at the central dot
of your map, while I
have marched out from Mortehoe
to Morte Point and on
to the lighthouse,
following the path
as it follows the land
as it follows the sea.
Eyes wide open,
looking all round,
one foot after the other.

And I bring you back gifts,
back through my map
to the arrow-point
where you sit with your book.

A dozen seals laughing, I say,
just north of the Point.
Hanging precisely in the roar of sun-skitter

and wave-yearning.
Poised over the long empty
saltiness, heads pointed
and gleaming, watching me
watching them.

Eyes wide open,
looking all round,
placing one foot after the other,
I know myself welcomed
to this wild wide world.

And I hold my hands out,
left and right,
to skim joy, whipped
into a handful of froth,
from the rocks and the sea,
and bring it back, glittering,
for you.

RETURN TO PORTLOE
(for Hugh)

In the quiet at the end of this breath
in the cove at the end of this land
there is a soft gathering of jewels, gleaming,
and a white bed in a white room, dreaming.
And the cliffs burn with willow-herb
and streams sing clear under meadowsweet.

And surely you'll be there waiting,
waiting for me; waiting while the sea
scours you to make you well.

Instead, a fishing boat dances, salt-lively,

while a sun-dark man with curly hair
slices fish open with an easy knife
and his rubber gloves turn bloody
and the gulls wait hungry in the sun
in the cove at the end of my breath.

Susan Jane Sims

BRIC À BRAC

Life is all busyness;
death an evaporation
of our conscious thought

yet never clean, never tidy.

Our possessions
collected over years
are bagged up as *bric à brac,*

our hearths swept clean
before something else
can inhabit

the space in which we so feverishly burned.

David Slattery

GRIEFWORLD

Leaves form your lips to speak to me. Soundless words that I cannot understand. The wind in the valley kisses you but I cannot.... I see you in the rose on the arch, the last rose that has no business being here in December (what do I know!) ... there it is ... impudently stubbornly living still ... on my way back from the woods I see only four petals ... after another few dayweekyears, three ... now two, still two!... now a single browning petal and after several frostfrozen days. ...
You've gone

Note: this section is extracted from a longer piece

Rachel Smith

YOU TAUGHT ME DEATH

Too many pups in a litter and you'd knock
a few on the head while we kids
made toothpick crosses for pet rabbits.

We played under the *rimu* tree, beside the stump
where every evening you chopped dog tucker,
sheep-fat catching in the grooves the cleaver made.

You at dusk, home from lambing, sack tipped out
in the kitchen, hard little hooves skating
on lino, us learning how to mix the milk.

Years later I'm home. It's winter. We chop
wood, stacking it under the *rimu*.
That night the phone rings.

You bank up the fire, make sweet tea,
sit with me as I wake friends.
For days and months you hold me.

STILL TRUE

No matter which way I look
it is still true. No matter
what angle, still true.
Forget for a moment,
put it down, pick it up,
still true. Shake my head,
wait for the relief of waking,
keep waiting.
Still true, still true.

SELF-RELEASE

At Pony Club we learnt
the self-release knot: one tug
and the halter-rope was free.

You were good at knots,
anything with thread or string.
Wounds stitched deftly. Wild flowers
on linen, back of the cloth
neat as the front.

Damn your neatness. Your ability
to calculate length.
To tie a knot that wouldn't slip.

Pauline Stainer

AFTERLIGHT
(i.m. my daughter)

I chose the liquidambar tree
knowing it would light
its own dying,
like those wasted children
wrapped in gold foil
to keep them warm.

Each autumn
when leaves fall
with the first frost
not even the kings of Persia
wore such saffron-yellow shoes
across the glimmering fallow.

I use them –
the colours of grief
like the mirror
in the cat's eye
to throw back
the single topaz at your throat.

Averil Stedeford

GONE–NESS

I cannot say you *have* gone
as if you might come back.
You used to be in one place at a time.
Mostly I knew where.

Now I say you *are* gone
Your absence walks with me.
So many empty spaces wear your shape.
There's gone-ness everywhere.

AFTERMATH

Grass growing after mowing or harvest

Look at my field.
Each day it's growing greener.
When the Reaper took you
he left stubble, only fit for burning.
No refuge, even for a rabbit.

Dry grief turned to tears.

Now ideas sprout, projects flower.
Your death has set me free
to grow a different crop.
It is unspeakable
but the green blades whisper:
I'm almost glad you died.

In this bright sky
dancing in the puddles
your reply?

Did you say: *So am I?*

Jonathan Steffen

AGAIN

Under my hand you hurtle, silken and fangsoft
Bright brindle boxer, deliriously dewlapped,
Playing the predator, playing the prey,
Seeking the certainty of another *again* –
And *again* and *again* and *again* and *again;*
Reminding me, half-absent human,
Of my own bounding brindle, for whom the great game
of *again* and *again* stopped long, long ago.

THE COLOUR OF GRIEF

I do not think that there is a colour for grief.
No black or grey,
No icy blue or putrid green or acid yellow
Could express the feeling.
It is like having ashes in your mouth
And gravel in the skin of your palms.
It is like weeping with every pore of your body.
It is like freezing all the way
From the centre of your heart
To the furthest edges of the universe.
Grief has no measure, no shape, and no horizon.
Perhaps only an artist
Who could create a colour that is beyond all colour
Could depict the colour of grief.

IN THE CHAPEL OF REST

I come to speak and have no words to say:
What words of mine could now be heard by you?
For I am here, and you are gone away.

I knew that I would live to see this day,
Yet, now it's come, I can't believe it's true –
But this is not what I have come to say.

I shan't speak. I shall find some other way
To do the thing that I have come to do.
And what is that? To come, and go away...

A thought occurs: Why don't I simply stay?
If you are here, then I can be here too!
And if I stayed all day, what would I say?

It seems I have the hardest part to play,
And shall be glad when this last act is through.
And timelessly the seconds slip away....

I saw my father: cold and dead he lay,
His looks, his face, his flesh I scarcely knew.
Is this the utmost I can find to say?
Dear God, why have you taken him away?

Jackie Steven

OUR MOTHER

Sharing space with our mother.
A tidy space, cats fluffed in contentment.
A warm feeling for us children.
Not everybody has it.

My father working
left us three females together.
So close and cosy
when not competing
for our mother's attention.
Then scrapping, pulling hair and biting.

My sister and our mother
had time alone now.
I was at school
wondering about what they were doing.
I was not concentrating. The nuns knew it.
Could try harder. Almost a plainsong.

They were black and white nuns,
sleek black and white cats
prowling down the corridors.
My days were filled with the holy spirit.
I went in procession
down to the grotto
through the witches' walk
of arched hazelnut trees
and then praying to Mary.

At home, I was tucked into bed at night.
A delicious time. Our mother
concentrating on both of us.

We said our homely prayers,
different from school's.

We seemed to embrace it all then.

We were young adults when our mother died,
(sorrow was unknown to us before).
She was in a coma.
We were all there together, including my father.
There was nothing to do.
We were really just waiting.
I sat near my mother
and prayed prayers from schooldays
beseeching our heavenly mother to help.
Pray for us now
And at the hour of our death. Amen.

Anne Stewart

GRIEF'S TRICK

My forehead has developed Dad's puzzled frown.
Skin and teeth make their own decisions.
Work passes. Time knows nothing
but presses in its murky marks,
smudges, shadows. Smoking's back
running its same old rings.

There's nothing the mouth can remember
of an honest smile. It does its best,
concocts a semblance, a responsive laugh
– brave mouth – braver than I am.
Did you know touch tells us more
than 70% of what we believe of life?

That frown – the fingers think they know
a trick or two, try to smooth it out, but Grief's trick
is better; he won't let my mirror see them go,
these vertical runnels, dreeping down.
Is this all it is to grieve? Cold confusion? This
dipping in and out of wish and thought?

This trying to dispel the shift of pain threatening
the heart? Wondering endlessly, did I say, did I do,
the right things? Did I listen well? When it came time
for counting, did he feel he could count on me?
This puzzled frown – this tight-lipped accusation –
what does it know that it's not telling me?

THIS STONE

will rise heavy and full under my hands.
It will carry the chill of church, the deep earthiness
of the old stone sink in Alloway I marvelled at
when I was young.

I see a dog, long-haired, black and white, turning
a scaled-down version of it in her great maw;
tossing it around, her teeth scraping at it
like a bite-sized bone.

It will have silver ridges set in, parallel lines
that travel upwards then deviate, slip over
its oval head, as fingers spread, rounding
a cheek-bone.

It will have pits and roughnesses my fingertips
will love and speak of lengths of stitches ripped
after a sewing job, a gift of resurrection,
has gone wrong.

More than anything, I will want to cradle
its height round shoulders in my palms, whisper
secrets to it. Things that only you and I
have known.

I will want to tell it how, once, years after,
when I stood by one of the unmarked graves
that might be yours, I talked uncertainly;
promised it a stone.

Greta Stoddart

NEUROBLASTOMA

So they were called to come in and watch
her moony thorax slapped up on the lightbox
show how a small shadowy gathering
had appeared in the dim garden of her lungs.

Home, and sitting at the long wooden table
where she'd lie to receive their daily trembling
dose of heparin, where now lay a Bible,
he said: *I want to be able to forgive them.*

Gethsemane. Moonlight. And the mob,
armed to the hilt, alert to the kiss,
who knew only what they had to do
and never mind who suffered
for how long or in how many ways,
came and took the beloved child away.

THE CURTAIN

Perhaps you know that story where people
step out of this world and into another
through a particular split in the air;

they feel for it as you would your way across
a stage curtain, plucking at the pleats,
trying for the folded-in opening through which

you shiver and shoulder yourself
without a single acknowledging glance up
to the gods, so keen are you to get back

to where you were before you made your entrance:
those dim familiar wings, you invisible,
bumping into things you half-remember

(blinded as you'd been out there
in the onslaught of lights, yes, blinded
but wholly attended to in your blindness).

Imagine our dying being like that,
a kind of humble, eager, sorrowless return
to a place we'd long, and not till now, known.

No tears then. Just one of us to hold
aside the curtain – *here we are, there you go* –
before letting it slump majestically back

to that oddly satisfying inch above the boards
in which we glimpse a shadowy shuffling dark.
And when the lights come on and we turn to each other

who's to say they won't already be
in their dressing-room, peeling off the layers,
wiping away that face we have loved,

unbecoming themselves to step out
into the pull and stream of the night crowds.

Jane Street

IT IS THE YEAR

It is the year for the grief of friends.
For the whisky bottle and prayers
From hearts that have seldom prayed,
And the lonely fight with destiny,
And bargains with God.

It is the year for the grief of friends,
For relinquishing the hopes of some day,
For watchfulness and the too spare
Comfort of clichés.

It is the year for the grace of friends,
For gallantry and games with words
In the last great confidence trick,
The year for small victories.
It is the year for the grief of friends.

Ajahn Sucitto

THE TURNING POINT

All those careful fluttering words –
dangling, wings caked with glue.
Let them struggle,
               let them
tip me out, cold.
                  What else is true
but fog and echoes? And
a door with no handle, neither open

nor shut. Its gape swallows
whatever I touch,
               owns everything.
So drop, just drop.

Into the widening pool.
An ocean,
where tides are turning.

Around a rocky point, they break;
with a glimpse of something silvery.
Then the wash of grey,
               again and again.

Beyond, soar temples of shadowless light.
Their threshold hovers –
distant, suspended.
               But certain.

Here the future doesn't pull,
and the blood is too old to push.
Here the point descends
               like a dove.

The loose ends
                  can dance their dance;
the reasons can work their way,
run clear to the riotous stars –

but out here the endings are stuck:
heart can't spin, mind won't weave.
Just a breath that flaps in my chest like a rag.

Until the point pries deeper – and something cracks.
You're gone.
And I'm left hanging one-hinged,
                              ajar.

THE BRIDGE

The stars are too old now.
Night's cool simplicity
drifts off, into distance.
The gleam of water, chatter-
chortle; mist's chill embrace;
razzle of birdsong. Tugged
and onrushing comes dawn.

The contrasts harden.
I'm leaned on a bridge,
fingers in stone.

The grit and the grain of it;
how it's stood, worked and set
arching the floods.
How it carries this lane –
which worms downtrodden,
gnawing the heels
of what's pacing inside me.

Compulsions and duties.
The sun claws the morning:
a cat toying with yarn.

The stream of non-endings
rolls in and rolls over.
But for a while I can lean here.
My reflection just hangs
in the stream, looking up:
a cluster of flakes,
dark in the laughter of light.

The bridge squats, absorbed:
the keeper of mantras,
humpbacked, flowing in true.

THE FIRE OF MY FATHER

The first fire against winter:
the stove prepared like an altar,
for an exorcism of the English damp.
I began with the old letters;

the gone voices, snatched and crumpled.
so I didn't hear the soft blue bird
didn't see till the paper rolled over,
the aerogramme kept twenty years

since he died. *Father.* Then his voice
calling out of the fire's mouth.
And again gone past my reach.
Dad, it's me out here, and I'm burning.

Tongue after flickering tongue
scoops up his chuckle, easy strength,

and safe, work-blunted hands.
And what we didn't, couldn't, say.

Running behind the watchful glass –
bright through this bone-cold dwelling,
his flames are free now, under my skin.
Father, here's your legacy:

this flare in the heart's crucible,
gusting and raging like a prayer
that's embodied; an eagle,
sacred, lifting, exultant,

that roof-bursts to ring the sky's bell.
Then let my history be smoke,
but its bent smudged finger
proclaims – among skies and earth,

and all that is bound in between,
shivering and burning: *Welcome.*
Because here is our home
on this pyre of lived days –

which I build with dead wood
to heat a small hearth. Pure
may it burn, purer than memory –
not to destroy, nor celebrate ashes,

but that hands might grow warm
by feeding it. And that heart
be worked, like rare molten gold,
from patience to a fathering grandeur.

Annie Taylor

FOR MYFANWY

You come to the gate to meet us
your feet on the sturdy gravel
treading as though on quicksands
keeping the gauzy air so still around you
no leaf remarks your presence; nor petal falls

With concentrated precision you hold erect
I have seen that intent balance
in tightrope walkers
their bodies centred with minute exactness
weighing Gravity and Grave

I embrace you with desperate care
afraid to press, to hold, to tilt
such fragile equilibrium
My husband, more impetuous than I
gives you the hug I'm terrified to risk

Our deliberately insouciant conversation
hops about, like sparrows in a branchy bush
We take your social reflection
from your eyes, probing no deeper
than you, or we, can bear

We respect your *façade* of ordinariness
and play your version of 'Truth, Dare, and Promise'
like obedient children
We are in your hands, and their circle
tailors our perimeters

The back of my throat aches
with the force of pent-up wishing. Silent pleading

that the evidence be disallowed
the jury re-consider
the verdict indefinitely suspended

David Thear

LEFT BEHIND

Suddenly he finds himself
on some distant shore,
and wonders how
it came to this.
Never alone before,
he seeks solace in the garden
but it's too soon to move on
from the hold in his life
that will not go away.

Aeronwy Thomas

DROWNING

Left on the seashore
we look at the carcase
stripped of all meat
bones blanched by the wind
and sometimes sun.
I want to touch it
to bring back life
that was,
to hear the mew of a sheep's cry
the other side of the estuary

where animals graze near the water's edge
the turning tide picking out one
to trap and turn in its pull and swirl,
water spiralling down.

This time it was a sheep.
Other times fishermen
mewl in distress
at the turn of the tide
dumped at the edge
of mud flats
once the waters cease foaming
a short-lived rage.
Sheep and men
caught in the tide
resurface in my dreams.

THE PARASOL

Today I saw you
on the sunny side
of the road
smiling and waving
high heels clicking
a pedestrian bumped you
and you crossed
to join me the other side
in a pool of gloom –
I shouldn't have spoken
about Mother's death –
made you remember
an urgent appointment
escaping in the nick of time
from the shady side
to enjoy the rest of the day

in full sun
a parasol to protect you
from its overpowering rays.

Sally Thompson

HOPSCOTCH

I am hoping
in a drawn
anxiety sort of way

Hopping from foot to foot
so I don't
touch
the ground
for too long

Who knows
if I keep
hop-scotching around the point
I may manage to miss it
altogether

And the white chalk squares
may contain all the pain and anger

So that when the rain
washes the chalk away

perhaps they will go
too

Martina Thomson

VISITATION

I left the asphalt path by chance
and there was grass under my feet,
soft and giving.

At once it was that spring-like world
with you alive and venturing.

I wore your coat and its familiar swish
stirred the breath of your walk;
in its pocket your dear hand.

I took a young leaf from a tree
and held it cool against my cheek,
bit into it to see you smile.

How close the wood-pigeon
on the branch above –
how slow and heavy its flight.

DAVID

Your chair I can touch now, it doesn't attack me,
your coat still hangs there but has no power.
All around here what there was is expended.
You don't disturb me. Perhaps I'm forgetting you.

But there's no safety on the roads beyond Galway
where snipers linger at crossroads – signposts
with names barely familiar target my chest.
Spiddal, Oughterard, Carraroe and Carna.

Sleepwalker, I'm drawn to the pub by the pier,

the one with the fish-shed askew beside it,
and on entering know we sat here –
I take the black drink of your absence.

Paul Hamo Thornycroft

YOUR VOICE SOMEWHERE COMES

Whenever you remember
Me
Or love
Or death,
A robin will sing.

Whenever you hear
The robin sing
You will remember me
And love
And death.

You will see the air
Divide before you,
The veil torn,
And in the peculiar light
A smile beckoning.

Isobel Thrilling

AFTER

When her husband died
she was
cold for weeks,
nets of shivers over skin.

Took on clothes,
her body grew fat with wool,
flesh shrank.

She tottered like a child,
hands faltered
over switches
handles and keys.

Adrift in new spaces,
odd creature
new-hatched from the
egg of grief,
bald, exposed, unfledged.

TRIBUTE TO ZUZANNA

She gave no platitudes like sweets,
count your blessings
is as useless as a humbug.

No exhortations,
no urgings to go for walks
or meet people,
no ersatz sweetness,
the world is grey to one

who grieves,
sunrise and sunset are ashes.

No music,
each note draws blood.

No advice about *letting go*
people are woven into
our fibres,
part of the living self,
not to be drawn from the psyche.

A silent touch on the hand goes
more than skin-deep,
she knew that
grief can go for the throat
or tighten the ribs;
that days will grow round the pain.

THE GRIEF-HOUSE

A place for the bereaved:
where people
know how to be with those
who grieve.

No lilies or hothouse blooms,
let it be warm,
muted light
with cushions of dusk.

No music,
such soundwaves disturb
the painful
dislocations in the psyche
like stroking a wound.

Small food,
and words depending on
those that
come from the broken throat,
no exhortations.

Quiet colours and voices
let the air
not flare with scarlet
or burst into virulent purple;
just spare
the occasional touch of a hand

Tricia Torrington

DESIDERATA
(at Langstone Harbour)

New Year's Day comes full of reversal.
The sky has leeched colour from the sea,
a wayward moon ghosting the day.

On my tongue flakes of ice,
forget the first winter of awareness
when snow touched me like this.

Will never forget when I kissed you
for the last time, just as now,
on your lips your frost and snow.

From the pontoon we pour you,
powdered like snow, into the water.
The pale sea claims you like a lover,

the breeze lifts you into blizzard,
we wait while cold seeps into bone,
while our words make the occasion.

You melt in the harbour like those crystals
on my tongue; I wait to leave until
the tide turns with all its ancient ritual.

Katharine Towers

THE WAY WE GO

the way we go about our lives
trying out each empty room
like houses we might own
eavesdropping for clues in corridors until

standing at a gate or attic window
seeing beauty in a flag of sky
we're gone, leaving the doors open
all the lights burning.

Suzanne Trevains

THINGS THE CHERRY TREE KNOWS

Everything rooted in change –
blossom, fruit, bare tree

Lucy Trevitt

BEING HUMAN

It is the way you hold your pain
in one hand
and your love
in the other

and bring the two
together.

You carry this truth
in a sheltered place
and collect joy and peace
in small doses

searching for the patterns
that reveal
the whole of things

affirming that
as a human being
you are, after all,

capable of the most tender
invincibility.

THE CONSTANT HUSH

Only the constant hush of water
Tells me I am unsleeping,
That, and the diminishing echo
Of a night bird calling

Could I be forgiven
For thinking it was you,
Watchful in the night about me?

The moon casts silver in a shimmering line
That runs across the water
Towards me,
Lighting up absolute darkness

Could I be forgiven
For thinking this was also you,
Watchful in the night about me?

There is nothing now but silence,
And for a second I see myself
As I might look from heaven,
A solitary figure,
Thin with grief and sadness

Like a shadow spilling over space,
Softly sighing when its secrets scatter,
Rippling outwards as they are touched
By the breeze

Could I be forgiven
For thinking this was you,
Remembering in the night about me?

Roger Turner

OLD MRS WINTERTON

When you get to heaven, you just won't know
old Mrs Winterton when you see her
for on that day,
the deep-set eyes and the old black coat,
the wrinkles and the crinkles
and the bittersweet smile,
the freckle-backed hands
and thick-stockinged feet
will all have been magicked away.

For God will have kindly remembered for her
the days of her beauty and youth –
she'll be wearing a shimmering deep red gown,
she'll be clutching the arm of a dashing young man,
flushed with love and money and wine,
as they were for those weeks along the Riviera,

and her dark eyes will be flashing,
and her feet will be dancing,
and her little white hands will entwine
with his, as they did at Menton and Ventimiglia.

And there she'll walk for ever,
saved, as if this was the truth –
not old Mrs Winterton, but young Amelia,

and she'll never remember how the young man will jilt her,
the scenes at the station, or the Paris train,
middle-class marriage, guilt and pain.

And so she'll walk for ever and ever,
under the palms at Ventimiglia.

THE MEN AT THE CEMETERY

It was the men who surprised me.
Of course, there were a few women, here and there –
white-lipped widows, all glamour gone,
hands careworn and poised,
fussing with flowers,
body language hinting at bitterness.
Lingering, last-looking,
till dull-eyed daughters drive them home.

But the men I had not expected.
In their fawn jumpers and roughly-ironed shirts,
their busy-ness hinting almost at cheerfulness.
They bring out their mowers, unload shears,
as if they were back home in the garden –
where, long ago they retreated
from some Boudicca of tidiness,
till habit became hobby.

They get on with the task
as if it was a work project,
almost-engineering, virtual-warfare.
Movement is continual,
clipping, mowing, hoeing:
to pause would let the enemy in.
They might notice heartbeats
juddering like uncertain gunfire,
regrets, jabbing like bayonets,
thoughts, sharper than the medic's needle.

A man comes pattering towards me,
plump, thick glasses, thin on top,
carrying dead flowers to the bin.
He asks me how I am.
Fine, thanks, I say.
It's a bad business, this, I add awkwardly.
But he prefers to talk about flowers, or the weather.

Soon grass and stone and flowers are in order,
clippers and shears go back into the car,
and he drives away.

But I'm new to this.
No stone yet,
not even the comfort of grass.
I linger, look back.
Drive off, silently.

Simon Tyler

WHERE THE BROKEN SKY BEGINS

Where the broken sky begins
Starts the rain
On my stone-quiet road again

Where the broken thought begins
Comes the pain
Rolling on and over all again

Where the broken rhythm runs
I recognise
The melody that swells and dies

I cannot join the sky
I cannot change the song
I cannot counter why
Certain moments last much longer
Than the twinkling of an eye

Where the broken night begins
I separate
Then from now, but echoes resonate

Where the breaking dawn begins
A light shines through
A strength that binds us through our days
And Time, and hope, and love renew

Christine Vial

THE SCATTERING

Ashes rest dry and heavy
in my cupped hands
then – thrown high – fly

caught in the summer wind
that skims chips of bone over
the blank surface of the lake

and blows ash back into my face
where loss burns hot and wet
and feels as light as air.

CHRISTMAS SHOPPING WITH THE DEAD

My dead mother walks the aisles of Tesco's with me,
complaining about the chill from the freezer cabinets
and reminding me unnecessarily that – as an anorexic vegetarian –
she won't be eating very much Christmas dinner again this year.

My dead father waits slothfully at home, drinking black coffee,
smoking constantly and marking the John Wayne films
in the new *Radio Times*. He hopes I've spotted
the Jack Daniels flavoured fudge for his Christmas stocking

while dead Aunty Sheila is lurking somewhere in the spirits section
muttering about Baileys and Harvey's Bristol Cream
and clutching a pack of Value mince pies. Like my mother,
she is shocked by the price of everything.

It's exhausting shopping with the dead – though strangely comforting –
so I think I'll head off to the store café where my mum will complain
the cappuccino isn't hot enough and my dad (having appeared unexpectedly)
will slope off outside for a crafty Benson and Hedges until Aunty Sheila's
agoraphobia kicks-in and she has a panic attack by the reduced goods counter.

And soon I will go home
to our neat little house with just the two of us now. The old are dead and
the young scattered and even less real. We are no longer worn down by
their demands and strange ways. Our Christmas will be quiet and simple,
selfish and smoke-free, and empty as the grave. It's less lonely here in Tesco's.

CROSSING THE BAR
(i.m Aunty Sheila)

She is dying
and she knows it
and she doesn't know it.
She is waiting for someone to tell her
she isn't going to die.

Death has slowly made its way
down the line of her large Irish family.
She is third from the top (except for Rodney
who died young of blood-poisoning)
at the hop-fields in Goudhurst).
The top two have gone.
It's her turn now.
That doesn't make it any easier.
And now, in her crammed cramped studio flat,

she closes the curtains against the pollen and the light.
She cushions herself with a multitude of family photographs,
souvenir postcards, soft toys and cardigans,
and exists on a diet of chocolate digestive biscuits,
Harvey's Bristol Cream sherry and old films on tv.

She is old brave stubborn angry
eccentric obsessional – her knees are crumbling
metal pins hold her hips together.

She still has the bone structure that made her beautiful.
She still has the scars that created a life lived alone.

She's very feisty, your aunt, says the Macmillan nurse.
She still needs your help, says my sister.

And the little girl with a shock of auburn hair
in a shabby scrubbed frock
evacuated into an unfamiliar world
dips a wary toe into the big cold sea
scared lonely gathering up her strength

          she doesn't as yet know how to swim.

Janet Watts

IN THE HOSPICE

My neighbour, Mrs Vicky Tripp,
sits up straight
in the chair
by her bed,
eyes imperious in a lost face.

I've done wicked things, she says.

I hold her hands together,
cradled in mine.

A frail-boned bird, fallen
but alive,
quivers

quietens

listens

in the silence
that isn't

in the dying

that isn't

J S Watts

LEGACY

Death is a state of mind.
I know you dead,
But within my head you live
And are summoned by each simple act
That bears your name.

The hanging of washing,
The ironing of clothes:
I feel you at my shoulder
And what once irritated
Is now softly welcome.

I will carry you with me,
Not always as sharp
But always as loved
And when my turn comes,
I hope
Someone will care enough
To bear us both
Into tomorrow.

Christine Webb

CANNOCK CHASE

I'm trusting to your sense of direction,
because I'm useless, you said, as we set off

across toughened bracken, snatching trails of bramble,
clumps of silver birch, though since you laughed

I took no notice, gave myself to our talk,
watched light on your cheekbones, gripped your wide

palm in its leather glove as you waited to steady me
over a stile. So when we paused for breath

an hour later, with not a clue about where
to look for the turquoise Renault, corroding still more

in the late October dew, I saw that you'd meant it
and that among these replicating tremors

of leaf, knots of grass, bushes, shadows,
we were lost, though neither of us yet said so.

KNOWLEDGE

That moment suspended in the dull room
above the streets of the January town

(a branch pecked on the window, but the curtains
shut out the garden of dead chrysanthemums)

– undressing for each other the first time
all I saw was lit up by your body,

its gold and ivory. Such knowledge to bring away,
to carry wrapped through the streets, past naked trees,

into the school where heating pipes clanked and gossiped,
where blackboards expressed decorous equations,

where at the corners of corridors we might breathe in
to pass each other, but did not speak or glance

in case the doorways should break into leaf,
in case the books we carried should burst into flame.

NIGHT CALL

It's three a.m., the night service can't find us
and I've rung Kit, who can. *Don't hesitate,*

she told me once, *nurses work odd hours*:
so this odd hour – you're gasping, belly distended –

she's struggling with your catheter which still
won't draw. We wash you out again, we rock

and tilt you on the bed, pinch and elevate
the snaking plastic. At last it warms with yellow.

You pull hard on your oxygen, and grin:
Why not check the electrics while you're here?

A week ago, at full stretch on our wonky
kitchen steps, Kit fixed the ceiling light.

It shone a day or two, went bust again.

RESPITE

The ambulance arrived early.
I looked at the man's clean skin, neat ears,
at a tiny mole on the woman's cheek.
Can you give me twenty minutes, I said.
No, they said, *this is an emergency ambulance:
we have to be back on call in half an hour.*

I wheeled you shaking from the bedroom.
It will be all right, I told you,
but they picked you up wrong,
laid you on the stretcher on your back:
you couldn't breathe.
No, you cried on a gasp.
She can't breathe on her back, I said.
They turned you on to the wrong side.
No, you cried. *Stop,* you cried.
She can only breathe on her left side, I said.
They took you out to the vehicle
marked Royal Berkshire Ambulance Service
in green capitals.
I couldn't reach inside to tell you
I'd be following.

I didn't know the way to the hospice:
I drove behind the ambulance, too close to the bumper,
squeezing in at roundabouts, jumping lights,
the bag like a passenger beside me with your stuff
and the two pages I'd written the night before
(when it was calm, when you were asleep):
Medication. Daily routine. How long
you'd been bedbound. What you ate.
She is highly intelligent, I'd written at the end:
she understands what is happening to her.
It is not easy for us to say goodbye.

In the room they lowered you into a bed
while I tried again to explain your one position,
the only way you could get air into your lung,
and again with your tiny pool of breath you cried
No, no, and clutched the side of the bed
until at last they found the angle

and settled you into it
and took me away
and gave me a cup of coffee in a quiet space
where I watched visitors come and go
and saw that nobody minded if they were crying.

SEVEN WEEKS

Seven weeks today. A July wind
is tousling the trees, rumpling the garden.
I have written five letters, washed the sheets.
A mistake somewhere – I've not finished
the crossword. Sit with the sounds of Sunday.
Thrashing leaves. Cows. Planes. My own breath.

All week the air has burnt: it is breath
from a lion's mouth. No stir of wind
to brush the cheeks of the sixth Sunday:
silence quivers in the house, and the garden
shrivels, as if the season's finished.
I sort bed linen. There are too many sheets.

A week leafed with letters. I scan these sheets
about you, half alert to hear your breath
until the words remind me that it's finished.
So sorry to hear. Rain in the wind
hasn't enough weight to nourish the garden.
Bells clang dryly. It is the fifth Sunday.

I wake in your presence the fourth Sunday –
not lying passive between your sheets
but laughing, striding in the summer garden
your mouth full of kisses, and your breath
sweeter and stronger than the June wind.
Why did I wake before the dream was finished?

Ready to go. *I've nothing left unfinished*
you told me once. But now beside a Sunday
river I want you here to watch the wind
curving sails, to feel the hauled sheets
as the boats put about, to taste the breath
of summer gusting down from every garden.

The second week I meet you in the garden
sitting under the oak where you once finished
fixing the swing-seat; not out of breath
but quiet and absorbed, reading the Sunday
papers, glancing up, rustling the sheets,
pinning one down that flutters in the wind.

I look out at the garden that first Sunday
when everything is finished. I smooth the sheets
and listen for your breath. There is only the wind.

Tony Weston

LET THE MOMENT IN

A flare of cyclamen catches light. *That's right,*
I say, *draw back the clouds and let the moment in.*
Across the wall, beside the sink, sun stencils in
the window pattern at a slant, picks out, flake white
the highlights on the mixatap, which lifts its head

as if to strike. You echo this. Your arm, your elbow,
the silver bangle at your wrist ease the coffee-cup
towards your lip. You sip, then drink and glance at me
and smile and, for a golden second, cup and tap
and cyclamen and sink and you and me sit
in the precious picture plane a single perfect thing.
That's right, I say, though not aloud, *let the moment in.*

Wynn Wheldon

LAST WORDS

When I get out of here, she said
from her hospital bed
I'll have so much to write about.

The drugs made her ramble: Harold
Laski and Henry James figured.
She worried about her legs.

In that hive of going and ends
there were little corners
where nurses gathered, laughed, lived.

On the last day the sun shone;
brilliant blue. From her window
the river glittered through Hammersmith.

The matron lit up a Superking.
My sisters smoked with her.
We hadn't done this before, hadn't

had to wait for mum to die.
We nodded and yessed,
took turns by the bedside,

got drunk in the bar opposite,
the table clocked with bottles,
were sobered by ammonia

and her loved face, waxen now
and almost expressing satisfaction
as though the book was at last finished.

Frances White

THE GATE

It wasn't easy
leaving you
alone at home
so soon after.

In the mirror
I saw you
leaning over
the garden gate
as I drove away.

Don't come out
I'd whispered
and when you did
Go back in
or you'll get cold
though it was summer.

DAFFODILS, I SUPPOSE
(for Aeronwy)

As you didn't value 'things',
I can't remember you
with keepsakes or mementos,
but when pressed to name
your favourite flowers,
you thought and said,
Daffodils, I suppose,
so now I'm glad I asked,
I approve of those.

LULLABY

They told me I must say goodbye.
His birth was long and I was torn
but I still sing his lullaby.

He did not breathe. He did not cry.
I held him close to keep him warm.
They told me I must say goodbye.

Above white masks, they glanced awry.
In vain, I breathed into his form
but still I sang him lullaby.

They gave no answer to my *Why?*
The guilt was theirs who would not mourn
and told me I must say goodbye.

You must forgive, they seemed to sigh.
My heart was with the hushed new-born
I rocked in tender lullaby.

Now every May when swallows fly
white blossoms spread among the thorn.
They told me I must say goodbye
but I still sing his lullaby.

THE BLACK CUILLIN

What fatal error undermined your skill,
When you set off without a glance behind,
Upon the slopes of those forbidding hills.

Escaping to the mountains and their thrill,
With trusted friends you knew to be your kind,
What fatal error undermined your skill.

You ventured out alone to breathe your fill,
A short walk in the sunshine to unwind,
Upon the slopes of those forbidding hills.

The sea lay tranquil and the island still.
I wonder if their magic made you blind,
As hidden peril undermined your skill.

No one was there to see you fall and spill
Your youth and all the plans you had in mind,
Upon the slopes of those forbidding hills.

The Black Cuillin captured your free will,
and shrouds the jagged facts so we can't find
What fatal error undermined your skill,
Upon the slopes of those forbidding hills.

Rik Wilkinson

BABARELLA DAYDREAM
(BABA)
(i.m. Zoe)

I remember how I called him in the field.
He whinnying his greeting at the end of day.
Then with the buckled leading rein close held
I'd walk him up the hill; and often speak
Your name and tell him of your letters home,
Hoping that *Zoe*, if repeated frequently,
Would fill his mind with you and he at play;
And stabled, he'd dream of gallops yet to come.

But you who loved his every ginger hair
(and grey ones too) who knew him better than
Oh, everyone had – at the end – to bear
The final brushing of his coat and mane,
Comb tail, wash hooves – be his most tender groom
And wish, and wish for him
                    green meadows in Elysium.

Chrissie Williams

MORNING AFTER
(i.m. Tony Turner 1933-2013)

Waking to a whisper of frost, knowing
there's none of your breath in the air today
I drift –
we're watching red kites in your garden, you say
even though the skies are full of them now
they still take your breath away.

Merryn Williams

THIS IS GOING TO BE ONE OF THOSE DAYS

When I don't cry. I've had
five out of thirty-one
with no tears at all. Not even
that faint, annoying prick
you sense at the back of the eyes.

I'm not going to listen to Handel's
Where'er you walk, or gaze
at certain photographs,
or play that video
which is trapped, and rotates in my head.

And if I get to six
p.m., I'll pour a drink,
congratulating myself
on having come so far.
It's not quite over. In bed
I'll pick up something light
and relaxing. Another day.

Wearing black now means nothing. The Victorians
did it for every fourth cousin. But I think
this sable suit appears – just one more outfit.
(My mouth is sandpaper. My eyes are ink).
They've no idea. If it could bring you back
I'd walk round all my life in swathes of black.

Emily Wills

RED PRIMROSES

I watch the sky: there is snow forecast.
You say you suspected for some time.

I carry shopping, satchels, books.
You arrange words and probabilities.

I am far away. I tidy rooms. I sleep.
You remember the three days we spent
on the cheapest bus to Greece.

I buy flowers and watch them opening.
You wonder how to tell the children.

I am shut inside. It is March
and should not be snowing.
The flowers are too red, the wind too cold.

The children are tight buds filled with words.
You will not see them opening.

You are shut inside. You watch the sky.
I feel I have known this for all time.

You tidy rooms. You sleep. You are far away.
The snow is too red, the flowers too cold.

INTO THIN AIR

Another sunrise, effortful and grey
begins it all again, this slow ascent
from bed to chair, from meal to meal,
with footholds that might give way
at any moment, and a small hammer
in her good hand to chip away
at almost unremembered things.

They bring her flowers which can't survive
this altitude, tall stories of some place
they think she knows. Reception's poor,
just snowstorms, static, noise.
They leg it carelessly, as if they haven't seen
gulley or icefall, been face to face
with rock. She doesn't know

who's roped above her, pegging on
or just about to fall. Three sides of her
is space she daren't look round on.
She wonders if this fraying rope
will last, she hopes the break
when it comes, is clean.

SWEATER

Knitted so loose it grew longer
at every washing, not *navy,* exactly,
rather a bruised sea deepening,
a dark you'd rather not
dive into, and now so drenched
with the salt-sweat smell of him,
so burred with brambles and griefs
she couldn't let it go. Months later,
trying it on for size, it muffles my hands,

and I'm pulling the wool over my eyes,
knowing it falls to me
to shoulder her face, that white torn gasp
as if she saw it all again, her gaze precisely
the colour of the sea that called him.

COVE

High tide, there's nothing but black rock, green swell,
so only locals can believe in a path, forecast
this half-ebbed tongue of sand. Imagine a holiday –
snap of a day, all sandpies and sandwiches,

toddlers shrieking on the edge, and the elderly
baked brown, white capped, who submerge
daily from March to October, and float
dignified and far out, whiskery as seals.

It's a doze of a day, salt crisping on pink skin
as they bathe and bliss; just enough breeze
to cool it, just enough silver to dazzle,
and close their eyes. If I had been there

would I have kept watch, seen it sooner,
stopped him? But always someone is clambering
the limits of rock, perched like a gull on a ledge
of air, reeling in an imaginary line, just waiting

to catch on to something. And now these young men
scrambling out of the sea, plunging in, climbing
higher each time and laughing,
daring, doubting.

Even now, I could put an end to it,
before they hike up this unbearable
pause, before the *Surely he won't*
but he does, and we're all stopped

dead, stuck with this minute replaying over
and over as something unwinged flies,
falls, happens on rock,
comes face to face with water.

THE SILENCE AFTERWARDS

At this moment someone is saying they will
or won't, or that they're on the train, and a fast white
sirens, but the girl in the shower doesn't hear
as it happens somewhere every day.

Right now, a man buys a ticket
for a plane that might be hijacked, or a lottery
that will or will not wipe out his friends,
and a girl with a toddler puts small change in a bucket.

Today a woman somewhere has lost
everything, or merely keys, and broken down
on some hard shoulder. Somewhere else,
a soldier hears, hesitates, and almost doesn't

but choice has been trained out of him.

Right now, one man is still holding on
but not for much longer, and at the same time
someone in a fake fur coat does not know
what to say and says nothing, which is just as well

because three minutes is a long time, and some people
said it should be only one because of the veterans
and young children, and because it's too difficult
or too easy but in this minute now there is some silence

which does not happen every day.

Margaret Wilmot

BONE-MEAL, LEAF-MOULD

Grandma kneels by the lilies. One hand
gently claws the soil; her spoon is a wand.
Plants need feeding too, she tells me, *just like you*.
The callas glow. Ferns, marguerites,
pelargoniums, begonias bask in her care.
I squeak a stalk of sour-grass clean from the ground.
How do you know what they want, I ask,
when they can't say? But then I see
a dandelion-clock, and blow. Light
pours all around. I play and never
feel cold, mulched in this first air.

Soft leaf-mould mottles the wood floor
where we walk. The trees are bare,
and a chill wind has blown the thin membrane
of winter light sheer to transparency.
Help Thou me, Mother says aloud, as if
I were not here. I think of Grandma teaching her
her prayers, a child kneeling by the bed, mind free
in its own sky, and of the cumulus now gathering
in her head. She seems more frail since her fall.
Bone-meal − if only. How to nourish this soil?

We reach the lane, and the wind has dispersed
all cloud. *Help Thou me*, Mother says
again, quite simply, to God.

WHEN SHE DIED
(i.m. Myrtle)

things felt unfinished, life
still yearning for

her richer chance…

I sat with the letter in my hand, watching
the boys play with
their wooden train: track not

in a circle, or figure-eight, but with random
sidelines, angles; brinks

they plunged an engine off, so freely,
to swim

a sea of carpet.

Stephen Wilson

AMPUTATION CLINIC

That gravel-crunch as you reverse
  Out of my life each morning
Wearing a thin integument of casual-smart
  Soft-sculpture I watched go on.
Soon you'll be at your desk swallowing
  Frustration, trying to break bad news
Gently offering yourself, the messenger
  To be over-killed before I see you back.

I don't know how you tell a man
  He'll never walk or recommend

A metal hook to someone for a hand
  That won't caress again –
Worse (by far I'd have to say) for them,
  Yet your going makes me think
I could be waiting there outside the door
  Ready to show my stump.

YOUR LAST STORY

When I was young and couldn't sleep,
you told me about the Albert Hall
on Saint Cecilia's day; a vacant piano stool,
waiting page-turner. The fluttering hands
that entered through a skylight,
dropped like a gannet to open an arpeggio.

I'm at the bedside now and you're in pyjamas,
propped and heaving like a broken pump.
We've been here more than once,
the night scare, the fibrillation.
But this time it's different, oxygen
hissing from a cylinder and you

throttled by the tide's crescendo. The sea's
inked your lips indelibly blue, cold-fingered
your skin and widened the blacks of your eyes.
What story shall I tell? The undertow against
our clasped hands as you're tugged out
followed by white gulls, white water.

Dilys Wood

MARINA TSVETAYEVA IN MOSCOW, 1919

How quickly the partings were over,
his love-letters became paper,

run for a handful of flour, Marina,
plead with a famous author

for two potatoes – ah, with one sick child
and one crying with hunger

do we need to ask, darling,
what makes you howl like a wolf in winter?

What makes young poet, a young mother
an orphan on her way home

from the orphanage? Where is the frost-breath
from two mouths, Marina,

as you crept through the streets with the child? –
do you doubt the State will feed her?

do you doubt that the State will find bread
for the young poet's young daughter?

and do you recall, like a puff of air,
on a Moscow street-corner,

as if his lips had been an altar
that sent up sacrificial smoke,

the ardent vows of your departing lover
and all the rest, exiling themselves

lost in the steam of railway stations,
promising to fight for Russia's soul

elsewhere.... But you never, *never!*
believed his words or his eyes – but only

how quickly the partings were over,
the love-letters became paper.

ORPHANS

On the slow bus back from the Hospice,
I think of something tragic, something I googled,
turning today to Russian poets
with their gift for suffering: Tsvetayeva

on the steps of the British Museum
in a borrowed coat of coarse dark serge –
a lightning-conductor, grounding
the sorrows of poets through her own body

shaking after seeing Keats' notebook
in the glass case, his life writ in water....
I weigh her pain, the guilt that grieves us both,
imagine her walking through Moscow slush

with the daughter she gave to the orphanage:
she left, believing carers fed the children;
at home she had three rotten potatoes
and one more child. It wasn't easy

to sit with you in the ambulance
as we ground our way to the pleasant building
with its neat lawns and its kind helpers,
walking to the door with you, as our frost-breath

floated up like sacrificial smoke....
So I force my mind to other times
and places: a mother's white breath higher
than a two-year-old's small breath, as they walked.

IN THE CHAPEL

We gather here, grieving and guilty: the two emotions inseparable.
Like climbers on a garden wall, the way such feelings twist into each
other, grow matted, can't be disentangled, surprises us yet again. The
question is: *What should we have done differently?* The excuses are valid
and not valid. Illness and dying happen within life. Life, as we say, must
go on. Some of our gestures and the actions were paltry – the quick
phone-calls, the unsuitable *Get Well* card from the nearest shop, using
the weather as an excuse not to visit.... We grieve for ourselves that we
should be so selfish: afraid of hospitals, afraid of *catching something*, afraid
of harrowing sights when we reach the ward and push those swing-
doors. We feel our own complications, inadequacy. When, at last, we saw,
but this is important! thrust other things aside, visited and talked to my
sister, it was a relief. She was human. She was grieving, guilty. She found
excuses to explain why she was dying.

COMPARING A WEDDING WITH A FUNERAL

We don't come here often. They've got white lilies again and the choir's
paid for, but it's very different. I was here for a wedding a month ago.
I seemed to be up there with the bride and groom, ready to leap into
the get-away-car, off on honeymoon. When I heard they were staying
the night here, I didn't approve, I thought: *No, get away on your own,
somewhere sunny, exotic* ... I warmed myself at their fires. Today I remain
very detached. Detached from the cold here, as I put on several layers.
Detached from the people who are letting themselves go, weeping. The
parson's detached, too, on this occasion. He got real warmth into his voice

blessing the married couple. Now his words are thin, he's waiting to get through it, get the hands shaken, get to the eats, a modicum of booze.... You can feel the shuffling, the denial, the coughing – oh that's a real grave-yard cough, poor woman! The daughter – she was the main carer – looks out of it, as if she scarcely knows what's happening, what might lie in the coffin ...You never get the same detachment at weddings.

Anna Woodford

MEMENTO MORI

The flame stands
for all your flown birthdays,
gilding your cake
with a fire the smallest
breath could smother.
Now it takes all your strength
to blow your wish. The day loses
some of its sparkle. I glimpse
how much dark one candle
can leave
before the nurse
clicks on the light.

Lynne Wycherley

REACH

Black filigree, the naked trees
stretch up through banded skies

cirrus streaks, small cumuli
trailing their grey-lit tides.

I search, I strive; I am the child
who never walked a world

bereft of you. How can I
thank you for all you've given?

The bare trees reach
through a hundred heavens.

MARY SHELLEY IN GENEVA AND LERICI

It came in a dream, a summer of rain.
Did they tell you how it happened,
the bet? Hairstreaks of light,
my creature stung to life,
shaking me with my own invention?

My child, my child, pushed
over cobbles, heaved from the shore,
butterfly lungs pressed flat.
Not a birth but an ice-bath
axing my senses with a scarlet flood.

Where am I in these waters?
The bay soothes us. Now placid, now restless,
returning my face. Flashes sunlight,
tourmaline, as Percy turns from
the window, lit with vowels.

There are tremors in the house tonight,
firelight in ebony. Albe is here.
They spark each other, hurl comets
across the room. I wane
behind glass as their dawn sails glide.

And now the shock – as if the sea
had miscarried. My husband
limp as sea-wrack. I was not at the burning:
I was numb. Somewhere in snow
my creature stumbles, searches.

Notes: ice-bath – to staunch miscarriage
Albe – Byron

BY A SAXON GRAVE

(i.m. Ian)

She's melted almost to nothing,
a femur's twig, a cranium's boll.
A brooch for each vanished shoulder.
A buckle to pierce the darkness:
a verdigris moon.

Discs and pins, art's precision –
not even such craft could hold her,
clothe her bones. She slipped free
from her skeleton's fern.
Glass beads and girdle-key
still beckon to be touched.

What shall we store, my love,
what tactile trace install?
Place against our pastel flesh,
clavicle, humerus, when
night's wave starts to fall?

Beach-stones, perhaps, from Rozel cove,
a seed-pearl for an ear-ring
as if time was a raindrop
hung in light; or our two rings,

twin annuli, their curl of love
candescent as the sun?

What shall we store though we
melt to silt, when breath has flown
from bone and bone's half gone?
Be brave, my love,
and take my hand

for the little sleep and the long.
The kiss you settle
in this hair, the tear,
will dazzle on a higher arc.
Signet. Kuiper belt. Star.

WAKING TO FROST

Now my calendar has shed its last leaf,
will I wake up to an unprinted meadow,
a future fanning out like snow?

I could populate such space with hope,
dream that no dark forest will set
its prison-bars between us and the sun.

Tomorrow, perhaps, the disillusionment,
heart's hangover, watching the world
reel round on its axis of pain

but today the grass is tipped with frost.
It piques my senses, reflects
a thousand points of light as if

God walks on winter's glass. I gaze
at starbursts, the shrapnel of disbelief.

BY THE FORTY-FOOT DRAIN

The Fens

Loneliness. The nail of the wind.
The dyke's antimony
stretching for miles.

A black road in suspension,
black fields below,
wheel-tracks ghosting off the edge.
Sometimes I'd hear
stories of fatalities,
grey cats of fog

stalking the fen,
winch-cranes stooping
over fallen metal bodies.

This road reminds me
of times of pain –
taut, uncertain, too tense to sustain –

earth to my left, water to my right,
whether I would drown
in darkness or light.

Alan Wynne Davies

THE LONELINESS OF BEREAVEMENT

The loneliness stays with you,
Looking at you;
Locking you in solitude,
And never goes away.
In a crowd it screams for everyone to hear
That you're alone.

But no-one listens,
No-one looks,
No-one stops
No-one cares;
Except those who have known and can understand
The void that's left behind,
The space in the bed,
That used to be a source of warmth.
The empty seat at the table,
That used to be your best friend,
Lover and companion,
Conversation partner; the whole world,

Beginning and end,
Night and day,
Light and dark,
Ocean, land and sky.
No-one can share that lonely place and
Only time can dull its sharp and tender boundaries.

Jeremy Young

POST MORTEM

A week after he died
the same nurses
were distracted
by the same demands
from others.

The specialist
was as absent
from her gratitude
as he had been
from her husband's fear.

She caught the bus
to bitterness
clutching
an empty bag
which had held her thanks.

SNOW

Once snow floated down
like delicate soft feathers,
covering the graphite skeletons
of trees with a thick
white layer of eiderdown.

We sat in the sun-room
all through that miraculous afternoon
watching the flake by flake transfiguration
of the dying world
to a perfect bright beauty.

You have stepped through the glass
and run away across the lawn
leaving only your crisp footprints
slowly melting
in the winter sun.

THE VOCABULARY OF HOPE

There are no words
      for a mother's grief
though some may come to birth
and stutter quietly before falling silent
      like the child she mourns.

Words creep away from pain
      in embarrassment,
or else they stand in antique clothes
at the graveside perched
      precariously on a heap of earth.

There are no words in the coffin.
      The vocabulary of hope
is as tentative as a small child
clinging to her mother's hand
      on her first day at school.

Martin Zarrop

RITUAL

Auden was right about suffering,
how it takes place as men in overalls
down all-day breakfasts
and study their mobile phones
while someone weeps at a nearby table.

As usual, the afflicted are left
to stumble through
Yes, I'm bearing up, thank you
and to wake early the day after
and the day after that
with their lists of mundane tasks.

How comforting to start
with a Tesco fry-up,
laughter, a chat about
nothing in particular.

I tick the boxes, keep on talking,
confuse false with true, dreaming
that the moon is cheese,
the earth is flat
and Icarus flew.

Pam Zinnemann-Hope

TODESENGEL★

My mother is back from holiday.
I am cutting roses for the table;
my mother is beside me.

> *I dreamt your father*
> *had another woman*, she says.

I am cutting the roses for the table.

> I can't believe
> the pain of it

The roses are double, pink fading to white.
I am cutting them
from one of the bushes
at the end of the garden.

> *I had to get up,* she says,
> *and smoke a cigarette*
> *while your father slept.*

I am cutting them with the left-handed
scissors with the orange handles,
a bouquet of small thornless roses
that grow in clusters

> I sat there for two hours.

I am cutting the roses from
the other side of the bush.
The soft petals are brushing my skin,
falling through my fingers.

★ *Angel of Death*

344

℘ BIOGRAPHICAL NOTES ℘

For reasons of space some of these notes have been lightly edited.

Shanta Acharya was born in India. She won a scholarship to Oxford, where she completed her doctoral thesis in English before going to Harvard as a Visiting Scholar. Her latest poetry collection is *Dreams That Spell The Light* (Arc Publications, 2010). She was elected to the board of trustees of the Poetry Society in 2011.

Ann Alexander has published three collections of poetry: *Facing Demons* (Peterloo Poets, 2002); *Nasty, British & Short* (Peterloo Poets, 2007) and *Too Close* (Ward Wood, 2010). She won first prize in the Mslexia, Frogmore, Bedford Open and Grey Hen competitions. She lives in Cornwall.

Zeeba Ansari is a poetry tutor. She has worked in partnership with Cornwall Adult Education and Library Services, and on a freelance basis. Her first collection, *Love's Labours*, was published by Pindrop Press in 2013.

Sara-Jane Arbury was born in Exeter and lives in Ledbury. A writer and performer, she has collaborated with organisations including the Arts Council, BBC, Oxford University Press and Bloodaxe Books. She is the former Voices Off Director at Cheltenham Literature Festival, and her poems have appeared in pamphlets and anthologies.

Aileen Armitage is a well-established novelist, never stopped by her blindness, who married Deric Longden when his first wife, Diana, died and became the perfect match for him. She survived him when he died in 2013.

Alice Audsley grew up in rural north Essex, an unsung part of England, where her formative years were steeped in little fields, hedgerows, woods and expansive skies in all their seasons. In adult life she has lived in Somerset, another beautiful county where the natural world remains a constant delight.

R V Bailey's poetry collections are: *Course Work* (Culverhay Press, 1997), *Marking Time* (Peterloo Poets, 2004), *Credentials* (Oversteps Books, 2012), *From Me To You* (Peterloo/Enitharmon, 2007) with U A Fanthorpe. *The Losing Game* (Mariscat, 2010) was written following the death of her long-term partner the poet U A Fanthorpe.

Anne Ballard is a retired family solicitor and Co-ordinator of Highgate Poets. Her poems have appeared in *Acumen, The Interpreter's House* and other magazines, and have been placed in a number of competitions including Poetry on the Lake 2011 and Barnet 2012. She is currently working on her first collection.

Wanda Barford was born in Milan and left Italy with her parents when Mussolini's Racial Laws came out. She settled in Southern Rhodesia (now Zimbabwe) and learnt English, a language she loves and esteems. Having published five volumes of poetry with a sixth forthcoming, she believes: *poetry is music written with words.*

Judith Barrington has published three poetry collections, most recently *Horses and the Human Soul* and two chapbooks, *Postcard from the Bottom of the Sea* and *Lost Lands.* She won the 2012 Gregory O'Donoghue Poetry Prize (Cork International Poetry Festival); her memoir, *Lifesaving* won the Lambda Book Award, 2001. She teaches classes and workshops in the USA, England and The Almassera, Spain.

Michael Bartholomew-Biggs is a retired mathematician living in London. He is poetry editor of the on-line magazine, *London Grip,* and also a co-organiser (with Nancy Mattson) of the reading series, Poetry in the Crypt. His poetry has been widely published; his latest collection is *Fred & Blossom* (Shoestring, 2013).

Heidi Beck emigrated to the UK from America in 1998. She holds MAs in both English Literature and Creative Writing. A member of the Bath-based Knucklebone Poets, she reads regularly with the Bath Poetry Café and has poems in their anthology, *The Listening Walk.*

Nikki Bennett has read in UK, USA and Europe. She believes in poetry as communication and therapy, highlighting women's issues. Her poems have appeared in various magazines and she has published six book collections and two CDs. *Love Shines Beyond Grief* was nominated for the Ted Hughes Award for New Poetry 2010.

Judith Benson works as a volunteer at the East Ham Nature Reserve as part of Green Gym (BTCV). She was Writer in Residence at the Dumfries and Galloway Royal Infirmary from 2004 to 2007. Her fourth collection of poems, *Hole in the Wall,* was published by the Rockingham Press in 2013.

Zanna Beswick is a university lecturer, director and consultant in drama and theatre. For British television she has commissioned and/or produced over 300 episodes of broadcast drama and has trained a stable of writers and editors. Her poetry has been published in journals, anthologies and in *The Independent.*

Elizabeth Birchall began writing poetry after a career in social work; her work has been published in various anthologies and magazines ranging from *The North* to *South,* and from *Acumen* to *Rialto.* A wide ranging medley *In Praise of Bees: a Cabinet of Curiosities* will be published in autumn 2014.

Vivienne Blake discovered poetry in her seventies, during an Open University Creative Writing course. She is making up for lost time, with poems published in anthologies and magazines, including *Long Story Short, Equinox, The French Literary Review* (in English and French). Vivienne lives with her retired dentist husband in rural Normandy.

Patrick Bond lives in Lewes, Sussex. He is a passionate admirer of the poetry of John Clare, and is a student of Thomas Traherne. His poem, *Printing Press No 379,* won the Torriano Poetry Competition in 2013.

Pat Boran was born in 1963 and lives in Dublin, Ireland, where he works in publishing and broadcasting. He has published five collections of poems, as well as *New and Selected Poems* (2005) and his prose works include *The Portable Creative Writing Workshop* (reissued 2013) and a memoir, *The Invisible Prison* (2009).

Pat Borthwick has twice been awarded Hawthornden International Writing Fellowships. Competition successes include winning the Amnesty Human Rights Prize, the Keats–Shelley and Basil Bunting Poetry Awards. She is currently completing OPEN, her fourth full-length collection. Pat is a Creative Writing tutor, a Stanza representative for Rural Yorkshire and former Chair of NAWE.

Stephen Boyce lives in Winchester. His poetry has been published widely in magazines, journals and online. He is author of two collections, *Desire Lines* (Arrowhead Press, 2010) and *The Sisyphus Dog* (Worple Press, 2014).

Sue Boyle runs the Bath Poetry Café and the associated Café Workshops and Writing Days. *Too Late for the Love Hotel* was one of the winning pamphlets in the 2010 Poetry Business Book & Pamphlet Competition, judged by Sir Andrew Motion.

Alison Brackenbury's latest collection (her eighth) is *Then,* (Carcanet, 2013). New poems can be read at her website.

Sarah J Bryson writes small poems and short stories, reflecting on life and death. She takes photographs nearly every day and works as a hospice nurse, part-time. Her work has been placed in competitions and published in various forms: in anthologies, in journals and on line.

Denise Bundred trained as a paediatrician in Cape Town and a paediatric cardiologist in Liverpool. In 2011 she completed an MA in Writing. She has had poems published in *The Hippocrates Prize Anthology* in 2012 and 2013. In October 2013 she read with Rebecca Goss at the Manchester Literature Festival.

Elizabeth Burns has published four collections of poetry, most recently *Held* (Polygon, 2010). Her poem in *The Book of Love and Loss* is part of a sequence of elegies, published as *The Shortest Days* (Galdragon Press, 2008), which won the inaugural Michael Marks Award for Poetry Pamphlets.

David Burridge has been writing poetry for about ten years. He has had various poems published most recently in *Orbis*. Now retired from a career as an HR Director and Employment lawyer, he uses poetry to record and explore people and situations he encounters in everyday life. A recent brush with cancer informed his poem in this anthology.

Robbie Burton has been published widely in magazines and anthologies. She runs Cross Border Poets, a Poetry Society Stanza, in North East Wales.

Maggie Butt's four poetry collections are the sumptuously illustrated *Sancti Clandestini – Undercover Saints*, the poignant *Ally Pally Prison Camp*, the pocket-sized *Petite* and the many-shaded *Lipstick*. Maggie is an ex-journalist, BBC TV producer and chair of the National Association of Writers in Education; she is based at Middlesex University.

Richard Carder's poetic appetite was enlivened by an inspiring teacher in his sixth form at school, where he was entranced by the sparkling rhythms of G M Hopkins. His subsequent poems have usually been inspired by Green issues, often arising out of work for Friends of the Earth. He has been convening the monthly Poetry and a Pint group since 1999.

Jennie Carr lives with her husband in West Oxfordshire. She lived and worked in New Zealand for several years but returned to the English countryside where she loves to walk, run and write.

Caroline Carver is a National Prize winner, Hawthornden Fellow, and poet-in-residence with Plymouth University's Marine Institute. She grew up in Jamaica and then worked in Canada as broadcaster, journalist and consultant before returning to the UK. She has published four collections to date, and has several projects waiting impatiently in the wings.

Rosalie Challis studied modern languages and spent the 1970s in France, working as a secretary, teacher and book consultant. Later, she joined *The Good Book Guide* in London, becoming a Director and Associate Editor there. In 2013 her poems appeared in *The Listening Walk* anthology and *Domestic Cherry* magazine.

Gillian Clarke, poet, playwright, editor, translator (from Welsh), was appointed the National Poet of Wales in 2008. Tutor on M. Phil course in Creative Writing, the University of Glamorgan, she is also president of Ty Newydd, the writers' centre in North Wales, which she co-founded in 1990. In 2010 she was awarded the Queen's Gold Medal for Poetry.

Rachael Clyne, psychotherapist and writer from Glastonbury, attends Wells Fountain Poets Group. She was a prize-winner in the 2012 Bath Acumen Competition and Sherborne Literary Festival. Publications: *ImPress* magazine and Bath Poetry Café Anthology – *The Listening Walk*. Collection: *She Who Walks with Stones and Sings* (P S Avalon, 2005). Her most recent pamphlet is *Singing at the Bone Tree*.

Claire Coleman has had a quirky working life as a teacher, street performer, clown, juggler, Fool and youth worker. She has poems in Bath Poetry Café's publication, *The Listening Walk*, and in The Fountain Poets' second *Anthology*. She is a member of Knucklebone Poets and regularly performs for the Bath Literary Festival.

David Cooke won a Gregory Award in 1977 and published his first collection, *Brueghel's Dancers*, in 1984. His retrospective collection, *In the Distance*, was published in 2011 by Night Publishing and a collection of more recent pieces, *Work Horses*, was published by Ward Wood in 2012.

Annemarie Cooper has had two pamphlets published: *Seeds*, by Flare Stack in 2000, and *The Flight of Birds*, by Soaring Penguin in 2013. She is an allotment holder, loves walking in nature, bird watching and reading, and is very interested in crop circles.

Wendy Cope read history at Oxford University and taught in London primary schools for fifteen years. She has been a freelance writer since 1986, when her first book of poems, *Making Cocoa for Kingsley Amis*, was published. Her fourth collection of poems, *Family Values*, appeared in April 2011.

Kay Cotton moved to Normandy after raising a family and working as an Educational Psychologist. She has poems in small magazines; in *A Speaking Silence* (a Quaker anthology), and more forthcoming in *Scintilla* and *The French Literary Review*. She is currently putting together a first full collection.

Martyn Crucefix has won numerous prizes including a major Eric Gregory award and a Hawthornden Fellowship. He has published five collections of poetry; the latest, *Hurt*, was published by Enitharmon in 2010. His translation of Rilke's *Duino Elegies* in 2006, was shortlisted for the Popescu Prize for European Poetry Translation. His new translation of Rilke's *The Sonnets to Orpheus* appeared in 2012.

Tim Cunningham was born in Limerick; he is a prize-winning Irish poet who now lives in England. He has published four collections: *Don Marcelino's Daughter* (Peterloo Poets, 2001), *Unequal Thirds* (Peterloo Poets, 2006), *Kyrie* (Revival Press, 2008) and *Siege* (Revival Press, 2012). His next collection, *Almost Memories*, is expected in October 2014.

Julia Darling (1956–2005) was a poet, novelist and playwright who lived in Newcastle upon Tyne. Her poetry collections, *Sudden Collapses in Public Places* (Arc, 2003) and *Apology for Absence* (2004) sought to open up the language around illness and healthcare, particularly breast cancer, from which she died in 2005. Her second novel, *The Taxi Driver's Daughter*, was long-listed for the Booker Prize.

Julia Deakin was born in Nuneaton and teaches at Bradford University. Widely published, she has won several first prizes and featured twice on Poetry Please. Her collections, *The Half-Mile-High Club* (a Poetry Business competition winner), *Without a Dog* (Graft, 2008), and *Eleven Wonders* (Graft, 2012), are all authoritatively praised.

Barbara Dordi writes poetry, reviews and articles. Formerly editor of *Equinox*, she now edits *The French Literary Review*, publishing poems, stories and articles with a French connection. Her latest collection, *Moving Still*, was published by Cinnamon Press; her latest bilingual poetry, *Les Joyaux d'Alfred*, was published in 2013. She lives in the south of France.

Noreen Drake-Stoker was born in Co. Carlow, Ireland in 1944. She currently lives in Dorset where she taught for many years before retiring in 2005. Many of her poems incorporate a childhood experience of living with her grandmother in Co. Clare, plus later life experience of extensive travels with her recently deceased husband, Richard.

Ann Drysdale has published five poetry collections, as well as memoir, essays and a gonzo guidebook to the City of Newport. She has been a hill farmer, water-gypsy, newspaper columnist and single parent – not necessarily in that order – and she now lives in a mining town in South Wales.

Carol Ann Duffy, poet and playwright, was appointed Poet Laureate in 2009, the first woman to hold this office. Her many awards for poetry include the Somerset Maugham, the Whitbread and the Forward Poetry Prizes. In 1983 she won the National Poetry Competition and in 2005 the T S Eliot Prize. She is Professor of Contemporary Poetry at Manchester Metropolitan University.

Jane Duran's collection *Breathe Now, Breathe* (Enitharmon Press, 1995) won the Forward Prize for Best First Collection. Enitharmon also published her collections: *Silences from the Spanish Civil War* (2002), *Coastal* (2005) and *Graceline* (2010). Together with Gloria Garcia Lorca, she translated Lorca's *Gypsy Ballads* (Enitharmon, 2011). She received a Cholmondeley Award in 2005.

Sarianne Durie wrote poetry when younger. She then went to Art College and made her reputation as a professional stained-glass artist. She had a great variety of commissions, sacred and secular. After her husband's death, she returned to writing poetry, still leaving time for her glass, garden, sheep and family.

Neil Elder's poems have been published in various magazines: *Envoi*, *Acumen* and *Prole* among them. The poem included here was one of several written in response to the death of his father. Neil lives and works in northwest London and is a member of Herga Poets.

Roger Elkin has won forty-five First Prizes and several awards internationally, including the Sylvia Plath Award for Poems about Women, and the Howard Sergeant Memorial Award for Services to Poetry 1987. His ten collections include: *Fixing Things*,2012, *Marking Time*,2012, and *Bird in the Hand*, 2012. Editor of *Envoi* (1991-2006), he gives readings, leads workshops and judges poetry competitions.

June English's first collection, *Counting the Spots* (Acumen, 2000) was short-listed for the BBC 'New Voices' programme. *The Sorcerer's Arc* (2004) and *Sunflower Equations* (2008) are both published by Hearing Eye. Her poems have been published in the *Daily Mirror*, (Carol Ann Duffy's Poetry Corner), *The Morning Star* and *The Guardian*.

Carrie Etter's poems here come from her third collection, *Imagined Sons* (Seren, 2014). She is a senior lecturer in Creative Writing at Bath Spa University.

U A Fanthorpe (1929–2009) published eleven collections of poetry. The first woman nominated for the post of Professor of Poetry at Oxford, she was *The Guardian's* chosen (but unsuccessful) candidate for Poet Laureate in 1999. Other honours included a CBE (2001) and The Queen's Gold Medal for Poetry (2002). *New and Collected Poems* came out in 2010.

Geraldine Farrow lives in a Dorset village and enjoys walking in its surrounding countryside; she also likes to catch a train and visit London. She has five children and four granddaughters who keep her busy and feeling young – most of the time.

Beverley Ferguson has a background in the Arts. She has taught Tai Chi and practised as a psychotherapist in Bath. Beverley is a founder member of the Centre for Whole Health and a founder member of Community Arts Therapies. Her experiences of mental illness inform her creativity as poet, writer and artist.

Victoria Field is a writer and poetry therapist, now living in Canterbury, after many years in Cornwall. Her third full poetry collection, *The Lost Boys*, was published by Waterloo Press in 2013. She is a playwright and a former Associate Artist at Hall for Cornwall.

Anthony Fisher started writing poetry in the early nineties and thinks of himself as a lyric poet drawing on his experiences for inspiration. He is a Fellow of the Royal Society of Chemistry and his pamphlet, *A Reek of Alchemy*, concerns a small eccentric business in Enfield as well as the area of Brimsdown. He is practising reading his poems whilst playing the guitar and is steeling himself to perform to an audience.

Rose Flint is an artist, an art therapist and a poet. She teaches creative writing and works in healthcare using poetry as a therapeutic medium. Her publications include *Mother of Pearl* (P S Avalon, 2008), *Nekyia* (Stride, 2003), *Firesigns* (Poetry Salburg 2004) and *Blue Horse of Morning* (Seren 1991).

Kate Foley lives partly in Amsterdam and partly in Suffolk, where she writes, performs, leads workshops and, when she can, works with artists in other media. Her seventh publication, *One Window North*, was published by Shoestring Press in 2012.

Angela France's poems have been published in many of the leading journals and have been anthologised a number of times. Her publications include *Occupation* (Ragged Raven Press, 2009), *Lessons in Mallemaroking* (Nine Arches Press, 2011) and *Hide* (Nine Arches Press, 2013). Angela is Features Editor of *Iota*, and she runs a reading series, 'Buzzwords'.

Wendy French has two collections: *Splintering the Dark* (Rockingham Press, 2005) and *surely you know this* (Tall Lighthouse, 2009). She won first prize in the Torbay Poetry Competition in 2008, and in 2010 won the NHS section in the Hippocrates Poetry and Medicine Competition. With co-writer Jane Kirwan she wrote *Born in the NHS* (Hippocrates Press, 2013).

Leah Fritz is an American ex-pat in London. Her earlier works comprised two prose volumes on political movements in the States in the 1960s and 70s. Her fifth and most recent poetry collection is *Whatever Sends the Music into Time: New and Selected Poems* (Salmon Poetry Ltd., Ireland, 2012).

Cynthia Fuller was born in Kent but has lived in the North East since the 1980s. She currently teaches creative writing at the University of Newcastle upon Tyne. Flambard Press published five books of her poetry, and her sixth collection will be published by Red Squirrel Press in 2015.

Ray Fussell is a retired company director living in North Wraxall. He came to poetry late in life and has been mentored by Sue Boyle of Bath's Poetry Café. He is now a member of The Knucklebone Poetry Group in Bath. He is married with two sons and six grandchildren.

Rory Gale, an aspiring young writer of prose and poetry, divides his time between Guildford and the South of France where he teaches English as a foreign language in Marseille. He was moved to this poem by the stroke his father suffered when his son was fifteen.

Katherine Gallagher is a widely-published, Australian-born poet, resident in London since 1979. She has five full-length poetry collections, most recently *Carnival Edge: New & Selected Poems* (Arc Publications, 2010) – its natural territory the exotic and unknown, the fringe and carnivalesque (Poetry Review). She translates from French and was a Parnassus Poet in 2012.

Frances Galleymore is both poet and novelist. Her poems have been published in *Orbis*, *South* and *South Bank Poetry*, and in *Peloton*, *The Ver Prize* and Highgate Poets' *Urban Harvest* anthologies. She won the 2012 Battered Moons Competition, and was shortlisted for the 2013 Keats-Shelley Prize.

Chrissie Gittins' poetry collections are *Armature* (Arc, 2003) and *I'll Dress One Night As You* (Salt, 2009). She writes radio drama and her short story collection is *Family Connections* (Salt, 2007). Chrissie's three children's poetry collections are all PBS Choices; two were shortlisted for the CLPE Poetry Award. She is listed in the Poetry Archive.

Geoffrey Godbert has fifteen collections of poetry/essays, and his *Collected Poems* was published in 2007. He is co-editor of two Faber poetry anthologies and editor of an anthology of Prose Poems for *Stride*.

Dawn Gorman has an MA in Creative Writing. She has published two poetry collections, *Looking for Gods* (Community of Poets Press,1997), and *This Meeting of Tracks* (one of four chapbooks in *Mend and Hone* (Toadlily Press, 2013). She co-organises monthly Bradford on Avon Words & Ears poetry events and the associated annual international poetry competition.

Rebecca Goss, who grew up in Suffolk, returned to live in the county in 2013, after spending twenty years in Liverpool. Her first full-length collection *The Anatomy of Structures* was published by Flambard Press in 2010. Her second collection, Her Birth (Carcanet/Northern House, 2013) was shortlisted for The 2013 Forward Prize for Best Collection and won the Poetry category in The 2013 East Anglian Book Awards.

Beverley Gray for some years attended Julia Green's inspiring creative writing classes. It was during this time that she produced the lovely villanelle reprinted here in her memory, following her early death; the poem is also in memory of the difficulties recently experienced by flood victims in Bradford-on-Avon, where she lived.

Philip Gross' *The Water Table* won the T S Eliot Prize in 2009. *I Spy Pinhole Eye* was Wales Book of The Year 2010, and *Off Road To Everywhere* won the CLPE Award for Children's Poetry, 2011. His recent collections *Deep Field* (Bloodaxe, 2011) and *Later* (Bloodaxe, 2013) dealt with his father's final years and loss of language.

Ruth Hanchett has always enjoyed writing prose, sometimes for publication – including an autobiographical book supported by a *Mind* Award. Now, a relatively new but older poet, she has had some poems published in anthologies and on line. She belongs to various poetry groups including Palmers Green Stanza and the Second Light Network.

June Hall lives in Bath, married to the novelist, Greg Hall. She has published two collections, with Belgrave Press: *The Now of Snow* (2004) and *Bowing to Winter* (2010), and is at work on a third. Her first baby's death and her own diagnosis of Parkinson's in her 40s have contributed to the birth of this anthology.

Katherine Hall is a struggling young professional with an unfortunate liking for champagne. Since poetry doesn't pay, she currently works for a marketing agency in central London.

Richard Hall lives in Seville, where he is teaching English as a foreign language and getting his head round Spain, Spanish and Spaniards. Between the sunshine and the challenge of climbing mountains, he squeezes in some writing, influenced by both family and new surroundings.

Sophie Hannah, who is also a novelist and children's writer, has published eight collections of poetry, as well as a *Selected*. In 2004, she was named one of the Poetry Book Society's Next Generation poets. Her poems are studied at GCSE, A-level and degree level across the UK.

Peter Hawkins is a writer, teacher and consultant, and is Professor of Leadership at Henley Business School. He was founder and previous Chairman of both Bath Consultancy Group and Bath Centre for Psychotherapy and Counselling. He lives with his wife on 37 acres at Barrow Castle on the edge of Bath where he leads workshops and provides spiritual and writer retreats.

Pippa Munro Hebden taught English for many years (her first Head of Department was U A Fanthorpe). She began writing for a Certificate of Creative Writing from Lancaster University. She enjoys writing poetry, short stories and memoirs, and is also a freelance theatre reviewer for a group of newspapers in the North West.

Marianne Hellwig John is married to the sculptor David John, and has six children. She has been painting for over fifty years and writing poetry seriously since joining a University of the Third Age workshop in 1991. She finds the two arts complement and feed into each other.

Diana Hendry has published six poetry collections, and over forty books for children, among them the Whitbread Award-winning *Harvey Angell*. A tutor for Arvon Foundation courses, she also reviews for *The Spectator*. She has been Writer-in-Residence at Dumfries and Galloway Royal Infirmary, and was most recently a Royal Literary Fund Fellow, based at Edinburgh University.

Michael Henry lives in Cheltenham and has had four collections published by Enitharmon Press, the most recent, *After the Dancing Dogs* (2008). In 2011 he won the Hippocrates Open Competition for a poem on a medical subject. A new collection is being finalised.

Gaia Holmes is a free-lance writer who works with schools, libraries and other community groups throughout the West Yorkshire region. She has published two poetry collections, *Dr James Graham's Celestial Bed* (Comma Press, 2006) and *Lifting the Piano With One Hand* (Comma Press, 2013).

Joy Howard lives in West Yorkshire and is the founder of Grey Hen Press. She edits and publishes anthologies featuring poetry by older women, organises frequent readings across the country and runs an annual competition. Her own poetry has been widely published in magazines and on line. Her latest collection is *Refurbishment* (Ward Wood, 2011).

Frieda Hughes was born in London; she is a painter, and a writer of poetry and children's books. *Wooroloo* (Bloodaxe, 1999) was followed by *Stonepicker*, *Waxworks*, *Forty-Five* and *The Book of Mirrors*. From 2006–2008 Frieda wrote the weekly Times poetry column.

Nora Hughes was born and grew up in Belfast. She moved to London in 1972. She has had poems published in a number of journals and is now working towards a collection.

Rosie Jackson lives in rural Somerset, writes, paints and runs workshops. Her poetry has been published in *Acumen, Ambit, Poetry Salzburg, Tears in the Fence*; it has been set for GCSE, and made into a sculpture in Dorchester. She has written four books: *Fantasy: the literature of subversion* (Routledge, 1981), *The Eye of the Buddha* (Women's Press, 1991), *Frieda Lawrence* (Harper Collins, 1994), *Mothers Who Leave* (Pandora, 1994).

Jennifer Johnson's poems have been published in several magazines including *Acumen, The Frogmore Press, The Interpreter's House, Obsessed with Pipework, Orbis, Poetry Salzburg Review, The SHOp, South* and *Stand*. Her pamphlet, *Footprints on Africa and Beyond*, was published by Hearing Eye (2006).

Hilary Jupp was born in Derbyshire. For the last forty years she has lived in Devon and South East Cornwall, where she worked in Mental Health Care. Her poems have appeared in *Equinox, Smiths Knoll* and *Poetry News*.

Jackie Kay was born in Edinburgh. She is a poet, playwright, novelist and writer of short stories and has enjoyed great acclaim for her work for both adults and children. Her novel, *Trumpet*, won the *Guardian* Fiction Prize, and she has published two further collections of stories with Picador, *Why Don't You Stop Talking?* and *Wish I Was Here*. She lives in Manchester.

Ann Kelley survived inadvertently snorkelling with sharks in Australia, walking into a pride of lions in Zimbabwe, and a close encounter with thirty elephants. She lives on a Cornish cliff and has survived a lightning strike, a landslip, a roof blowing off, and a large double-glazed panel descending on her. She nearly played cricket for Cornwall.

Lisa Kelly is a half-English and half-Danish writer. Her pamphlet, *Bloodhound,* was published by Hearing Eye (2013). She has been shortlisted for the Bridport Poetry Competition, and was published in Poetic Republic's eBook of winners, 2012. She is a regular host of poetry evenings at the Torriano Meeting House in London.

Mimi Khalvati has published seven collections with Carcanet Press, including *The Meanest Flower*, shortlisted for the T S Eliot Prize. *Child: New and Selected Poems 1991–2011* was a Poetry Book Society Special Commendation and *The Weather Wheel* is due in 2014. She is a Fellow of the Royal Society of Literature.

John Killick was a teacher for thirty years, and has been a full-time freelance writer since 1989. He has been a small press publisher, and has published two collections of poetry, and written two self-help writing texts with Myra Schneider. In the dementia field he has written five books and edited six poetry collections.

Wendy Klein was born in the United States but has lived in England most of her adult life. Published in many magazines and anthologies, she has two collections from Cinnamon Press: *Cuba in the Blood* (2009) and *Anything in Turquoise* (2013). She is convinced of the curative qualities of dancing, dog ownership and reading poetry.

Kaye Lee is an Australian poet who lives in north London. After working for forty years in health care she retired, and can now spend more time writing. She has been published in poetry magazines and anthologies, and has been a prize-winner in several competitions.

Pam Leighton's thirty-year teaching career encouraged her love of reading, writing and sharing all genres of literature. She wrote her first poem, *White Wave*, about the sea when she was ten and since then has written poetry ceaselessly. Now at 80 she feels she is just getting into her stride.

Tim Liardet has produced nine collections of poetry with two more forth-coming from Carcanet. His various awards include an Arts Council England Writer's Award, five Poetry Book Society Recommendations and Special Commendations, A Whitbread Prize long-listing and T S Eliot Prize short-listing. He is Professor of Poetry at Bath Spa University.

Maxine Linnell was a novelist, poet and psychotherapist until her son Benn died suddenly in 2010. He was 37. Life is slowly recreating her. She's loving her small grandson, beginning again as a psychotherapist, and writing a book about sudden death in epilepsy. She lives in Leicester.

Deric Longden married **Aileen Armitage** in 1990 following the death of his first wife, Diana – subsequently made famous in Deric's bestselling *Diana's Story*. He found another very special person in his second wife, who became the perfect match for him. Deric died in 2013.

Bernard Lord retired from work as a GP to France, where he enjoys the challenge of a new language. *Almost Tomorrow* is part of a sequence written whilst caring for his terminally ill sister-in-law. His collection *Floating Stones* (Perigord Press, 2012) was launched at the St Clementin LitFest, Deux-Sèvres 2012.

Janet Loverseed feels lucky, having two children, six grandchildren and a partner who encourages her writing. She has been published in a number of magazines and anthologies and has been a prize winner in both the Virginia Warbey and Grey Hen competitions. Her pamphlet *The Under-Ripe Banana* was published by Happenstance (2008).

Rupert Loydell is Senior Lecturer in English with Creative Writing at Falmouth University, the editor of *Stride* magazine, and the author of several collections of poetry, including *Wildlife* (Shearsman Books, 2011), *Ballads of the Alone*, and *Encouraging Signs*, a book of essays, articles and interviews (both books also published by Shearsman Books, 2013).

Gill McEvoy, a Hawthornden Fellow, has published two collections, *The Plucking Shed* (Cinnamon Press, 2010) and *Rise* (Cinnamon Press, 2013). She collaborates with singer Polly Bolton to produce 'sung and read' shows. She has published two pamphlets with Happenstance Press (2006, 2008) and a third pamphlet, *Philomela*, is forthcoming (Happenstance Press, 2015).

Joan McGavin is an Associate Lecturer in Creative Writing at the University of Winchester. Oversteps Books published a first full volume of her poems, *Flannelgraphs*, in 2011, and in 2012 she received a Hawthornden Fellowship. She is a Trustee of the new Winchester Poetry Festival, and is Hampshire Poet for 2014.

Lachlan Mackinnon's most recent collection of poems is *Small Hours* (Faber). He has written four books of poems, two critical books and a biography, and reviews regularly for the national press. After thirty years of teaching, he now lives in Ely.

Denise McSheehy's work has been widely published and also broadcast on BBC radio. Her collection *Salt*, funded by a major Arts Council bursary, was published by the Poetry Can (2008). She has received an Author's Foundation Grant towards her next collection. She currently lives in Devon.

Ruth Marden is a retired English teacher living in Salisbury. Her main focus has been on literature in schools in this country, but at odd times she has taught EFL, and she worked for two years in Switzerland and nine in Greece, which she regards as her second home.

Alwyn Marriage has been a university lecturer, chief executive of two NGOs and Editor of a journal. Three of her seven published books have been poetry. She is Managing Editor of Oversteps Books, holds a research fellowship at the University of Surrey and gives readings all over Britain and abroad.

Felicity Marris, born 1970, lives in Bristol with her four children. She has been published by *Equinox* and by Cinnamon Press; was long-listed for the Cinnamon Press Poetry Collection Award, and was shortlisted for the Plough Prize.

Deborah Mason was brought up in Barnard Castle and graduated from the universities of Leeds and Manchester. After working in Japan and Finland, she now works for Oxford University. She started writing poetry after she moved to Oxford, and since 2007 has been a member of the Back Room Poets.

Nancy Mattson moved from the Canadian prairies to London in 1990. She has three full-length poetry collections: *Finns and Amazons* (Arrowhead Press, 2010), *Writing with Mercury* (Flambard, 2006) and *Maria Breaks Her Silence* (Coteau, 1989); shortlisted for Gerald Lampert Award). She co-organises Poetry in the Crypt in Islington, London.

Tony Maude lives with his wife near Edinburgh, Scotland. He is a proof-reader/ editor and an ordained Baptist minister. In his spare time Tony is a team member at the dVerse Poets' Pub.

Anna Meryt has been published in many anthologies and magazines, most recently in Highgate Poet's Anthology (Feb 2013); a short story in Greenacre Writer's Anthology (May 2014). A performance poet for many years, in 2011 she won first prize in the Lupus International Poetry Competition. Her poetry collections – *Heartbroke* (Oct 2013) was recently reviewed in Gold Dust magazine and *Dolly Mix* were published by Tambourine Press (May 2014).

Joan Michelson's publications include *Toward the Heliopause* (Poetic Matrix Publishers, USA, 2011); poems, fiction and essays in the British Council anthologies, *New Writing*, vols. 3, 4, 14; poetry and fiction in magazines and anthologies in USA, UK, Israel, India, Romania. She won the Poetry Society's Hamish Canham Prize in 2012. Originally American, Joan lives in London.

John Miles' main claim to poetic fame is that he failed English Literature 'O' Level, and hasn't looked back since. After a lifetime in scientific pursuits, he now lives with his poet wife Suzy in a fuzz of theatrical obscurity in a charming retirement bungalow in Brixham, Devon, overlooking the mortgage.

Elma Mitchell (1919–2000) won first prize in the Cheltenham Literary Festival Poetry Competition in 1977. A professional librarian, she also worked in broadcasting, publishing and journalism in London. Her four collections, *The Poor Man in the Flesh* (1976), *The Human Cage* (1979), *Furnished Rooms* (1983) and *People Etcetera* (1987) were published by Peterloo Poets.

Andrew Motion taught English at the University of Hull before becoming Editor of *The Poetry Review*. Later he was Editorial Director and Poetry Editor at Chatto & Windus. He was Poet Laureate from 1999 to 2009, and is now Professor of Creative Writing at Royal Holloway, University of London. He was knighted for his services to literature in 2009.

Beryl Myers attended Camberwell Art School, worked as a potter and taught art subjects in Adult Education. Her poems have appeared in various publications and OU anthologies and she has published her own collection of poems, *Picked Up In Passing* (National Poetry Foundation, 2000).

Sylvia Oldroyd lives close to the New Forest, an area which has inspired much of her poetry. She has published three collections, including *A New Forest Calendar* (Brimstone Press, 2002), and *A Mouthful of Stars* (Brimstone Press, 2008), and is currently working on poems based on her family history.

Vicky Olliver first began writing poetry in 2006 following a knee injury which kept her off her feet. She has been a member of Highgate Poets for several years and is now starting to have poetry published. She is also interested in Zen Buddhism, gardening and travelling to mountains.

David Olsen won the Cinnamon Press Poetry Collection Award with *Unfolding Origami*, which will be published in March 2015. His three poetry chapbooks from US publishers are *Sailing to Atlantis* (2013), *New World Elegies* (2011), and *Greatest Hits* (2001). His work appears in journals and anthologies in Britain, US, Ireland, and France.

Jennie Osborne lives on the edge of Dartmoor. When not writing, she is a counsellor, specialising in loss and bereavement. Her collection *How to be Naked* was published by Oversteps Books in 2010. Co-author of the collaborative book, *Poets, Painters and Printmakers*, her work is widely published in magazines.

Katherine T Owen wrote/dictated prolifically during fourteen years bed-bound with severe ME.CFS. She is author of *It's OK to Believe*, (Presence Publishing, 2014), a poetic and narrative journey which challenges our ideas of faith and reason. Published in various anthologies, Katherine has given radio interviews, talks, readings and workshops and has a spiritual journey of healing website.

William Oxley has given readings throughout the UK, as well as abroad (Nepal, Antibes etc.); his poems have been widely published (e.g., *The New York Times*, *The Observer*, *The Spectator*, *The Independent*, *Agenda*, *Acumen*, *The London Magazine* and Poetry Ireland Review). His most recent volumes are *ISCA – Exeter Moments* (Ember Press, 2013) and *Collected and New Poems* (Rockingham Press, 2014).

Jeremy Page has edited *The Frogmore Papers* since 1983. His short stories have been widely published, and he is the author of several collections of poems, most recently *In and Out of the Dark Wood* (Happenstance, 2010). *Closing Time* is due from Pindrop Press later this year.

Mark Pasco, the youngest of five children and the father of three, works in the area of addiction as a probation officer. He and his wife live in Gloucestershire; he enjoys wooding, writing and helping to run a play site for disabled children.

Robert Peake is an American poet living in England. His pamphlet *The Silence Teacher* (Poetry Salzburg, 2013) was praised by Magma Poetry as an 'uneasy, affecting and unforgettable collection'. He founded Transatlantic Poetry on Air, pairing poets from both sides of the Atlantic for live readings online.

Pat Perry was born in Cornwall. For her, words have been the essence of her working life. Trained as a journalist, she has also worked in public relations and latterly as a counsellor, when listening to the words that are said and to those that are left unspoken is of equal importance.

Jo Peters lives in Yorkshire and is a retired teacher. She was encouraged to concentrate on her poetry after an Arvon course in 2009. She has been published in *Acumen, ARTEMISpoetry, The Interpreter's House, Pennine Platform*, and anthologies of poetry for children. She has won prizes in several competitions.

Mario Petrucci is a winner of the Arvon and Bridport prizes and the London Writers Competition (four times) and a PBS Recommendation. He has held pioneering residencies at the Imperial War Museum and Radio 3. War, science and ecology deeply inform his poetry. Mario was shortlisted for the 2012 Ted Hughes Award.

Ellen Phethean is a writer and editor. Her first collection *Breath*, (Flambard, 2009), was shortlisted for the London Fringe 1st Collection Award, 2010. Her second collection *Portrait of the Quince as an Older Woman*, is due to be published by Red Squirrel Press in 2014. Ellen runs workshops and teaches Creative Writing.

Nicky Phillips lives and writes in rural Hertfordshire. Her work has appeared in *The Cannon's Mouth; Wonderful World of Worders* (Guildhall Press, 2007); *Ink, Sweat and Tears; The Ranfurly Review*; and *Heart Shoots: an Anthology in aid of Macmillan Cancer Support* (Indigo Dreams Publishing, 2013), among others.

Dorothy Pope's 440 poem successes include publication in *Acumen, The Spectator* and *The Literary Review*. First prizes include: The Poetry Society's Canham Award and the SWWJ's (four times). Two self-published books, *The Fourth Man* and *The Summerhouse Poems*, will shortly be followed by *A Mile of Kite String*.

Sue Proffitt lives in South Devon. She has been writing poetry all her life, and is now putting together her first collection. She has M.A.s in English Language and Literature and in Creative Writing, and her work has been published in *South, Scintilla, ARTEMISpoetry* and *Ariadne's Thread*, and in two anthologies: *Confluence*, (Leaf Books, 2010) and *Moor Poets Volume 3* (Moor Poets, 2013)

Jay Ramsay is the author of 35 books of poetry, non-fiction, and classic Chinese translation. His latest publications are *Agistri Notebook* (KFC, 2014), *Keys to the World* (Waterloo Press, 2014) and *Shu Jing – the Book of History* (Penguin Classics, 2014). Poetry editor of *Caduceus* magazine, he also works in private practice as a UKCP accredited psychotherapist and healer.

Jeremy Robson A leading figure in the poetry world of the 1960s and 70s, and for many years the *Tribune* poetry critic, he also edited a number of anthologies, including *The Young British poets* (Chatto) and, with Dannie Abse, the *Corgi Modern Poets in Focus* series. His own most recent collection is *Blues in the Park* (Smokestack Books, 2014).

Mark Roper's most recent collection, *A Gather of Shadow* (Dedalus Press, 2012), was shortlisted for *The Irish Times* Poetry Now Award 2013. *The Backstrand*, a collaboration with photographer Paddy Dwan, was published in Autumn 2013. Eric Sweeney's opera, *The Invader*, for which Mark wrote the libretto, will be premiered in May 2014.

Michael Rosen Fifth Children's Laureate Michael Rosen is one of the best-known figures in the children's book world. He has written numerous award-winning poetry books, non-fiction and picture books.

Diana Sanders is a writer, musician and teacher. Much of her inspiration is gathered from the wild landscape of North Wales in which she lives. The hills, weather, wildlife, history and mythology are woven into the poetry, stories and music that she writes.

Geoff Sanderson wrote both poems in memory of his wife, Jill, at the request of St Michael's Hospice Chaplain, Harrogate, for an annual families' Memorial Service called *Light Up a Life*. Publication here is arranged by his daughter, Kate Sanderson, in memory of Jill whose roses are still going strong two years later.

Jane Saunders is a counsellor, psychotherapist and supervisor and she lives with her family near Bath. She has been writing poetry since her teens and has found it a great comfort in times of pain and distress. She is interested both in the creative nature of therapy and the therapeutic nature of creativity.

Linda Saunders' poems have been widely published in magazines and anthologies. She is a member of the International Association of Art Critics, and has eight grand-children. Her first full-length collection, *Ways of Returning* (Arrowhead Press, 2004) was shortlisted for the Jerwood Aldeburgh Prize; her second, *The Watchers*, is also published by Arrowhead Press (2009).

Myra Schneider has had several collections of poetry published. Her new book is *The Door to Colour* (Enitharmon 2014). Other publications include books about personal writing and novels for young poeple. She tutors for The Poetry School in London and is consultant to the Second Light Network of Women Poets.

Lynne Sedgemore CBE is a new voice of poetry for healing mystical expression and social justice. Her first collection *Enlivenment* is published by Chrysalis Poetry. Lynne wrote *Slipping Away* for her mother. She is a full-time Chief Executive, has a Doctorate in Spiritual Leadership and lives in Somerset.

Jill Sharp's poems have appeared most recently in *Mslexia, Fourteen* (final issue), *Poems in the Waiting Room, The Listening Walk* (Bath Café Poets), *In Protest* (Senate House) and online at *And Other Poems* and *Ink Sweat and Tears*. She tutors for the Open University and convenes a local writers' group.

Lindsey Shaw-Miller lives and writes in the nave of a converted chapel in the Mendips. She is creating a garden on a tiny plot, cultivating her library and preparing her first collection for publication.

Penelope Shuttle, literary consultant and Chair of Falmouth Poetry Group, lives in Cornwall and has published a number of poetry collections. Her most recent is *Unsent: New and Selected Poems 1980–2012*, Bloodaxe Books, 2012.

Pat Simmons worked in marketing and communications for a number of overseas development charities, including 13 years with Oxfam. Retirement has given her the opportunity to develop her poetry writing. In 2008 her husband Hugh developed oesophageal cancer, and she cared for him until his death a year later.

Susan Jane Sims enjoys encouraging adults and children to read and write poetry, through her publishing venture, Poetry Space, as a writer in schools for Threshold Prize, and through Lapidus. She is currently developing an interest in performing poetry and has read at Bath Literary Festival with Bath Poetry Café.

David Slattery has been writing poetry on and off since his teens. Now, forty years later, this trickle has become a steady flow, even a torrent at times! His writing is very influenced by the relationships with those he is close to (including nature) and draws on his twenty-five years as a psychotherapist and teacher.

Rachel Smith grew up on a farm in New Zealand. She studied Literature at Canterbury University NZ, before coming to London where she works as a chef. Her work has appeared in *The North*, and she has been a guest reader for the Shuffle (Poetry Society). She is a member of Tideway Poets.

Pauline Stainer has published eight collections with Bloodaxe. Her last book *Tiger Facing the Mist* was published in the spring of 2012. She is a Hawthornden Fellow, and a Cholmondeley Award winner. She is also an artist, and is interested in how word and visual image reflect one another.

Averil Stedeford is a psychiatrist, now 81, who worked for twelve years in an Oxford hospice. Her poetry comes from clinical work and personal experience, and she used it in teaching medical students and others. Such poems appear in the second edition of her book *Facing Death: Patients, Families and Professionals* (Sobell Publications, Oxford, 1994).

Jonathan Steffen was born in London in 1958 and read English at Cambridge. He is the author of the poetry collections *St. Francis in the Slaughter-House*, *The Colour of Love* and *Exposure*, as well as a CD of songs, *The Road in Our Feet*.

Jackie Steven has loved poetry since primary school when she heard beautiful poems on the radio during English lessons. She has loved writing since this time. Now she uses writing to explain the world to herself. At 68 she has more time to read and write.

Anne Stewart is a provider of services to poets and poetry organisations, principally through *poetry pf* and Second Light network. She has an MA (Dist.) in Creative Writing from Sheffield Hallam University, has won the Bridport prize, and her first collection is *The Janus Hour* (Oversteps Books, 2010).

Greta Stoddart was born in 1966 and grew up in Oxford. Her first collection *At Home in the Dark* (Anvil, 2002) won the Geoffrey Faber Memorial Prize and her second *Salvation Jane* (Anvil, 208) was shortlisted for the Costa Poetry Award. Her poem *Deep Sea Diver* was shortlisted for the 2012 Forward Prize for Best Single Poem. She lives in Devon.

Jane Street started writing poetry when she was married: later, no longer married and with a little more time, she followed her father and grandfather – both published writers – and wrote several novels, two of which have been self-published. But except for a haiku there have been no more poems.

Bhikkhu Sucitto (aka Ajhan Sucitto – Ajahn means 'teacher') is a Theravadan Buddhist monk and meditation teacher. He is currently based at Cittaviveka Monastery in West Sussex, and contributes to *Dhamma Moon* poetry website from where copies of his book *Travels In The Middle Land* can be downloaded.

Annie Taylor trained as an illustrator and textile designer, but later became an actress, working extensively on stage and in television. Her poems have been published in various magazines and anthologies.

David Thear was born in London and after university worked for ten years in magazine publishing before, with his wife Katie, setting up his own business in 1975. Living in Essex, he is now retired and has been writing poetry since 2010, after his wife died.

Aeronwy Thomas (1943 – 2009), was the daughter of the Welsh poet, Dylan Thomas. She taught Creative Writing and collaborated with a wide circle of artists and writers. Aeronwy published several collections of her own poetry and a memoir of her childhood in Wales, *My Father's Places* (Constable - London, 2009).

Sally Thompson is a barrister, mediator and writer. She trained as a classical pianist, studying at the Guildhall School of Music, and later went on to qualify for the Bar. She lives in London, practising from Chambers in the Temple. Her poetry has been published in various anthologies and periodicals.

Martina Thomson (1925-2013) was born in Berlin but left just before WW2 for London where she trained as an actor, and went on to act in BBC radio plays. In the late 70s she qualified as an art therapist; she also became an experimental ceramicist and a poet. Her work was collected in *Ferryboats* (2008), and in 2012 she published *Panther and Gazelle*, translations of the expressionist poems of Paula Ludwig.

Paul Hamo Thornycroft born in 1949 in Steep, Hampshire, brought up in rural Berkshire. Biological Sciences degree (University of Sussex). Sculptor, painter and writer. Lives in Stroud, Gloucestershire.

Isobel Thrilling was born in Suffolk and brought up in Yorkshire; read English at Hull University, spent many years as Head of Service for ESOL in a London borough. Widely published in magazines and anthologies from OUP, Longman and others. Poems on BBC and ITV tv and Radio 3 & 4. Many prizes, including Bridport. Poems used for GCSE English Literature.

Tricia Torrington is a poet and Fine Art printmaker living in Gloucestershire. She has had many poems published in magazines and anthologies, and has won a number of poetry competitions. Her first collection, *The Opium Fish*, was published by Flarestack in 2010.

Katharine Towers was born in London in 1961 and read modern languages at St. Hilda's College, Oxford. She has an MA in writing from Newcastle University. Her pamphlet *Slow Time* was published by Mews Press in 2005, and her poems have appeared in publications including *Mslexia* and *The North*. She lives in the Peak District with her husband and two daughters.

Suzanne Trevains lives in Bath and works as a psychotherapist. She is inspired by the idea that 'everywhere I go, I find a poet has been there before me'.

Lucy Trevitt is an artist, poet and facilitator of therapeutic support groups and creativity workshops. Living with chronic illness profoundly shapes her life and work, giving rise to a particular interest in the relationship between creativity and well-being, and an affinity with working with the thresholds of life and death.

Roger Turner is an architect, garden designer and author of five non-fiction books. His poetry has appeared in three collections: *The Summer Palace*, *Six Partitas* and *An Italian Notebook*. U A Fanthorpe said *Turner is that not-often-found-thing, a master of the sentence. His are like Hopkins' weeds, 'long, lovely and lush'.*

Simon Tyler started writing poetry at school. The themes of time, beauty and loss recur in his poetry, expressed in poems about love, landscape and the mysteries of our changing lives. Simon lives in Wiltshire and regularly attends the Bradford on Avon Poetry Workshop.

Christine Vial lives in Enfield, North London, where she teaches literature and creative writing and is a committee member of Palmers Green Poetry. Her work has been published widely, most recently in *The Interpreter's House* and *South Bank Poetry*, and she performs her work regularly, both locally and wider afield.

Janet Watts worked for *The Guardian* and *The Observer* in London for many years, writing interviews, profiles and features. But she fell in love with the Isle of Purbeck in her youth, and finally left London to live there. Free of newspaper deadlines and politics, she now writes poems in Purbeck.

J S Watts' poetry and stories appear internationally and have been broadcast on BBC and Independent Radio. A poetry collection *Cats and Other Myths* (2011) and an award nominated poetry pamphlet, *Songs of Steelyard Sue* (2012), are published by Lapwing Publications. A novel *A Darker Moon* is published by Vagabondage Press (2012).

Christine Webb's poems have appeared in a number of magazines and anthologies. Her second collection, *Catching Your Breath* – from which the five poems in this volume are taken – was published by Cinnamon Press in 2011, following *After Babel* (Peterloo Poets, 2004). *Seven Weeks* won the Poetry London competition in 2007.

Wynn Wheldon is a freelance writer. His prose has appeared in numerous journals, magazines and newspapers. He currently reviews books for *The Spectator*. His short fiction has won prizes and his poetry has been published in *Acumen, Ambit, London Magazine, Prole*, and *The Rialto*, among many other 'little magazines'.

Tony Weston Born Oxford, December 1941. Resisted all attempts at education. Fifty years of making and selling more or less useful pots in the Portobello Road, then in Cambridge. Married his Muse, Bundle. Together they remade a courtyard of buildings with glorious gardens. Retired to Dorset. Four volumes of published verse.

Frances White's poems have been published in two anthologies by a quartet of poets: *Away With Words* (Poetry Monthly Press, 2007) and *A Ring of Words* (Number 11 Publishing, 2012). Frances lives in London and has read her poems at The Troubadour, The Poetry Café, Rhythm & Muse, Lumen and the Torbay Festival of Poetry.

Rik Wilkinson has worked for the Ordnance Survey as a surveyor; he has studied English at Oxford, and taught English in Hertfordshire schools. His poems have been published in several magazines, including *Acumen Literary Journal*. In 2007 he was invited to be a guest reader at the Torbay Poetry Festival.

Chrissie Williams was lucky to find Metroland Poets when she started writing poetry over ten years ago. This led her to *South* poetry magazine readings, and to joining the magazine's management team. Her work has been published in a number of small press magazines and anthologies. She has recently moved to Bristol.

Merryn Williams was the founding editor of *The Interpreter's House*. Her third collection, *The First Wife's Tale*, was long-listed for the Welsh Book of the Year 2007; a fourth will be published by Shoestring Press in 2015.

Emily Wills has two collections: *Diverting the Sea* (2000) and *Developing the Negative* (2008), both published by *The Rialto*. Her work appears regularly in magazines and she won the Frogmore prize in 2012 and 2013. She lives in Gloucestershire where she works part-time as a GP.

Margaret Wilmot was born and studied in California. She taught English in various places, including the Mediterranean and New York City, before settling in England to raise a family over thirty years ago. *Smiths Knoll* published her pamphlet *Sweet Coffee* in May 2013.

Stephen Wilson is a psychiatrist and writer. His first collection: *Fluttering Hands*, appeared in 2008 followed by *Things Hard For Thought* in 2012. He has been a Hawthornden Fellow. His critical books include a study of the WWI poet, *Isaac Rosenberg* and *Poetics of the Diaspora*.

Dilys Wood, whose collections are *Women Come to a Death* (Katabasis, 1997) and *Antarctica* (Greendale Press, 2008) is the founder (in 1994) of the Second Light Network of women poets and the co-editor of five anthologies of poetry by contemporary women poets, including *Her Wings of Glass* (to be published in 2014).

Anna Woodford's poetry collection *Birdhouse* (Salt, 2010) was a winner of the international Crashaw Prize. She has received a Leverhulme Award, an Eric Gregory Award and a Hawthornden Fellowship. She has a doctorate in the poetry of Sharon Olds, and lives in Newcastle upon Tyne.

Lynne Wycherley was born by the Fens, and now lives by a headland. Love and landscape are keynotes of her work. Her new volume, published by Shoestring Press, is *Listening to Light: new & selected poems* (2014).

Alan Wynne-Davies would describe himself as an environmental poet, writing about landscape and places. He is a member of Back Room Poets in Oxford and performs in Open Mike nights and Slams.

Jeremy Young lives in the Somerset countryside where he is in private practice as a systemic psychotherapist. He has been widely published in magazines and anthologies in Britain and Ireland, including *Acumen*, *The Interpreter's House*, *Orbis*, *The Frogmore Papers*, *The New Writer* and *The Listening Walk* (Bath Poetry Café, 2013).

Martin Zarrop is a retired mathematician who wanted certainty but has found life more interesting and fulfilling by not getting it. He started writing poetry in May 2006 and is widely published in magazines and anthologies. He has an MA in Creative Writing from Manchester University and aims to generate a collection (sometime). Meanwhile he just wants to continue the love affair and keep on writing.

Pam Zinnemann-Hope's *On Cigarette Papers* (Ward Wood, 2012) was short-listed for the Seamus Heaney Prize. Pam subsequently adapted the book for the acclaimed Afternoon Play of the same name on Radio 4, in which she acted. She has performed at King's Place, London, among many other venues. She facilitates workshops, and has held many residencies.

INDEX OF TITLES

375

377

ꙮ ACKNOWLEDGEMENTS ꙮ

The poems in this anthology are reprinted from the following books, all by permission of the publishers listed unless stated otherwise. Thanks are due to all the copyright holders cited below for their kind permission.

Every effort has been made to trace copyright holders and include correct acknowledgements, and the editors apologise if errors or omissions remain in this list. They would be grateful to know of any corrections that should be incorporated into future editions.

Shanta Acharya 'Remembering' from *Shringara* (Shoestring Press, 2006); 'Somewhere, Something' from *Dreams That Spell the Light* (Arc Publications, 2010).

Ann Alexander 'Death is a big word' from *Too Close* (Ward Wood, 2010); 'To the front, as night is falling' (Grey Hen Press, 2013).

Zeeba Ansari 'Water' from *Love's Labours* (Pindrop Press, 2013).

Sara-Jane Arbury 'Grief' from *Bugged . . . Writings From Overhearings* (Bell Jar, 2010).

R V Bailey 'Travelling in the dark', 'Hands', 'At the hospice', 'Parts of speech', 'Finals', 'Hard work', 'Familiar' from *The Losing Game* (Mariscat Press, 2010); 'With you' from *Credentials* (Oversteps Books, 2012).

Wanda Barford 'Chattering' from *Losing Finding* (Flambard, 2002).

Judith Barrington 'What We Say' from *Horses and the Human Soul* (Storyline Press 2004).

Michael Bartholomew-Biggs 'Widower' from *Tradesman's Exit* (Shoestring Press, 2009).

Heidi Beck 'Instructions For My Heirs' from *The Listening Walk* (Bath Poetry Café, 2013).

Nikki Bennett 'Clothes Memories' from *Love Shines Beyond Grief* (The Poetry Spring, 2009).

Judith Benson 'Columbarium' and 'The Scent of Her' from *Call It Blue* (The Rockingham Press, 2000).

Zanna Beswick 'Always' from *Earth Ascending* (Stride Publications, 1997).

Elizabeth Birchall 'Parcelling Up the Crucefix' from *The Interpreter's House 50* (Interpreter's House, 2012).

Pat Boran 'Winter Burial', 'Obituary' and 'Let's Die' from *The Next Life* (Dedalus Press, 2012).

Stephen Boyce 'Stones' from *The Sisyphus Dog* (Worple Press, date).

Sue Boyle 'Widow' from *Too Late For The Love Hotel* (Smith Doorstep Books, 2010).

Denise Bundred 'Foetal Scan' from *The Edmund Cusick Avalon Prize* (Up To the Point Press, 2011).

Elizabeth Burns 'The Arrival' from *Held* (Polygon, 2010).

Robbie Burton 'Glose: Open Space' *Envoi: Issue 160* (Cinnamon Press 2011).

Maggie Butt 'Address Book' from *Petite* (Hearing Eye, 2010); 'Ice Rink' from *Quintana Roo* (Acumen Publications, 2003).

Gillian Clarke 'On the train' and 'A death in the village' from *Making the Beds for the Dead,* (Carcanet, 2004).

Rachael Clyne 'Terminal Conversation' and 'Tidying Drawers' from *The Listening Walk* (Bath Poetry Café 2013).

Wendy Cope 'Dutch Portraits', 'The Widow' and 'Spared' from *Family Values* (Faber & Faber, 2011).

Julia Darling 'Apology for Absence' and 'Indelible, Miraculous' from *Apology for Absence* (Arc Publications, 2004); 'End' from *Sudden Collapses in Public Places* (Arc Publications 2003).

Julia Deakin 'Prescription' and 'Codicil' from *The Half-Mile High Club* (Smith Doorstop Books, 2007); 'Lost' from *Without a Dog* (Graft Poetry, 2008).

Barbara Dordi 'With A Bang' from *Airing Cupboard* (Pamphlet Poets, 1999); 'Knowing' from *Moving Still* (Cinnamon Press, 2009).

Ann Drysdale 'Scattering His Ashes' and 'Winter Camping' from *Between Dryden and Duffy* (Peterloo Poets, 2005).

Carol Ann Duffy 'Cold' from *Poetry Review* (Summer 2009).

Jane Duran 'Hairpins' and 'Cape Porpoise, Maine' from *Coastal* (Enitharmon Press, 2005).

Neil Elder 'Grief-stricken' from *Red Ink 4* (The Incwriters Society, 2008).

Roger Elkin 'Marking Time' from *Marking Time* (Sentinel Poetry Movement, 2013).

June English 'Riversflow' from *Sunflower Equations* (Hearing Eye, 2008); 'Gathering Lilac' from *The Sorceror's Arc* (Hearing Eye, 2004).

Carrie Etter 'A birthmother's catechism' (September 11, 1986) from *Imagined Sons* (Seren Books, 2014).

U A Fanthorpe 'Song', 'The passing of Alfred', 'Tomorrow and…', 'Idyll', 'Elegy for a cat', 'Chaplaincy fell walk' and 'Queueing outside the *Jeu de Paume* in light rain' are all from *New and Collected Poems* (Enitharmon, 2010); 'Break' and 'The dying man and the lovers' are by permission of Dr R V Bailey.

Beverley Ferguson 'Illness' from *Winning Poem Poetry Space* (Poetry Space Ltd., 2009); 'Outpatients Appointment' from *Flowers in the Blood* (Poetry Space Ltd., 2014).

Victoria Field 'Forget-me-nots' from *Olga's Dream* (Fal Publications, 2004).

Kate Foley 'My Father, Counting Sheep' and 'Thrown' from *Soft Engineering* (Onlywomen Press, 2004).

Angela France 'Counting the Cunning Ways' from *Hide* (Nine Arches Press, 2013); 'Tell the Bees' (under the title 'Bereft') from *The Price of Gold* (Grey Hen Press, 2012).

Wendy French 'Three Years On', 'In Limbo' and 'City Road' (Hippocrates Press, 2013).

Cynthia Fuller 'Changes' from *Moving Towards Light* (Flambard Press, 1992); 'Time Travel' from *Instructions for the Desert* (Flambard Press, 1996); 'No Fairy Story' from *Background Music* (Flambard Press, 2009).

Katherine Gallagher 'Cloud-Eye' and 'The Long Reach Out of War' from *Carnival Edge: New and Selected Poems* (Arc Publications, 2010); 'The Long Reach Out of War' from *Passengers to the City* (Hale and Ironmonger, 1985).

Chrissie Gittins 'Registrar' from *I'll dress one night as you,* (Salt, 2004); 'There are things I must realise you can no longer do' from *Armature* (Arc Publications, 2003).

Geoffrey Godbert 'Remembering' from *Forget-Me-Not* (Berkshire Academic Press, 2012).

June Hall 'Bath-time', 'Bowing to Winter', and 'Yellow Bird' from *Bowing to Winter* (Belgrave Press, 2010); 'Anniversary', 'Truth Trail', and 'Untimely' from *The Now of Snow* (Belgrave Press, 2004).

Sophie Hannah 'Your dad did what?' was first printed in *Loving and Leaving You* (Carcanet, 1999).

Diana Hendry 'Dressing Mother' from *The Seed-box Lantern: New and Selected Poems* (Mariscat Press, 2013).

Michael Henry 'Funeral kiss' from *The Warwick Review,* (June 2012).

Gaia Holmes 'Peninsula' from *Dr James Graham's Celestial Bed* (Comma Press, 2006); 'All I Can Do For You Is Dream' from *Lifting the Piano With One Hand* (Comma Press, 2013).

Joy Howard 'Travelling North' from *Cracking On* (Grey Hen Press, 2009).

Rosie Jackson 'Having It All' from *Domestic Cherry 2* (Domestic Cherry, 2012); 'My Mother's Engagement Ring' from *The Interpreter's House* (The Interpreter's House, 2013); 'The Letter Cutter' from *Acumen* (Acumen, 2014).

Jennifer Johnson 'Missing' from *Stinging Nettles* (Nettle Press, 1998).

Hilary Jupp 'Mother Orchard Cotehele' from *National Trust South West Newsletter* (National Trust, 2003).

Jackie Kay 'The no-longer dead' and 'The bird' from *Fiere* (Picador, 2014)

Ann Kelley 'Fluent' from *Because We Have Reached That Place* (Oversteps Books, 2006); 'A Lump In The Throat' from *Paper Whites* (L.M. Editions, 2001); 'Telling the Bees' from *Telling the Bees* (Oversteps Books, 2012).

Lisa Kelly 'For Sale' and 'Homeward Bound' from *Bloodhound* (Hearing Eye, 2012).

Mimi Khalvati 'Prunus Avium' 'Tears' and 'What It Was' from *Earthshine* (Smith Doorstop Books, 2013).

Wendy Klein 'Clearance' from *Anything in Turquoise* (Cinnamon Press, 2013).

Tim Liardet 'The Dark Age', 'The Revenant', and 'Like Slant Rain' from *The Storm House* (Carcanet, 2011).

Bernard Lord 'Almost Tomorrow' from *In A Cerulean Sky* (J and G Simms, 2002).

Janet Loverseed 'The Lonely and the Sea' from *Running Before the Wind* (Grey Hen Press, 2013).

Rupert Loydell 'Further Than We Thought' and 'Namesake' from *The Smallest Deaths* (Bluechrome, 2006).

Lachlan Mackinnon 'At Maryculter' from *The Jupiter Collisions* (Faber, 2003); 'In Memory of Keith Darvill' and 'Small hours' from *Small Hours* (Faber, 2010).

Gill McEvoy 'When God Made Time' from *The Plucking Shed* (Cinnamon Press, 2010); 'Bread' from *Uncertain Days* (Happenstance Press, 2006).

Denise McSheehy 'How Would We Talk?' from *The SHOp* (2014).

Ruth Marden 'Yes!' from *Acumen 40* (Acumen, 2001).

Nancy Mattson 'Stash' from *Finns and Amazons* (Arrowhead Press, 2012).

Anna Meryt 'Heroes and Ghosts' from *Heartbroke* (Tambourine Press, 2013).

Joan Michelson 'Wife' and 'Sleep' from *Towards the Heliopause* (Madjock Press, 2008); 'Sleep' from *The Widow's Handbook* (Kent State University Press, USA, 2014).

John Miles 'Girl On The Seafront' *from In Case Of Fire, Throw This In'* (Vane Books, n.d.).

Elma Mitchell: 'Turning out the mattresses' from *People Etc.* (Peterloo Poets, 1987).

Andrew Motion 'The Mower' from *New and Selected Poems* (Godline, USA, 2009); 'Serenade' from *Public Property* (Faber, 2002).

Sylvia Oldroyd 'Coming of Age' from *South Issue 25* (South, 2002); 'Coming of Age' from *A Mouthful of Stars* (Brimstone Press, 2008).

David Olsen 'Vertigo' from *The Book of Euclid & Other Stories and Poems* (Cinnamon Press, 2013);

Jennie Osborne 'Hand-Me-Downs' from *How To Be Naked* (Oversteps Books, 2010).

William Oxley 'He Was My Prospero' from *Sunlight in a Champagne Glass* (Rockingham Press, 2009); 'A Charm Against Loss' from *In the Drift of Words* (Rockingham Press, 1992); 'The Gift of Your Ways' from *An Anthology for Patricia Oxley* (Rockingham Press, 2011).

Jeremy Page 'Fading' from *Acumen 46* (Acumen Publications, 2003).

Robert Peake 'The Silence Teacher' from *The Silence Teacher* (Poetry Salzburg, 2013).

Mario Petrucci 'Last words', 'Ark' and 'Stroke' from *Flowers of Sulphur* (Enitharmon, 2007). 'The Room' from *Heavy Water* (Enitharmon, 2004) and 'If you were to come back' from *Shrapnel and Sheets* (Headland, 1996).

Ellen Phethean 'Rowing Home' from *Breath* (Flambard, 2009).

Sue Proffitt 'Two Sisters' from *Moor Poets Vol. 3* (Moor Poets, 2013).

Mark Roper 'Silence', 'A Last Breath' and 'Public' from *A Father of Shadow* (Dedalus Press, 2013).

Linda Saunders 'Keeping the Fire' from *She River* (Vane Women Press, 1999).

Myra Schneider 'Leave Taking' from *The Panic Bird* (Enitharmon Press, 1998). 'Stillness' from *Circling the Core* (Enitharmon Press, 2008).

Lynne Sedgemore 'Slipping away' from *Enlivenment* (Chrysalis Poetry, 2013).

Jill Sharp 'Valediction' *14 Magazine Issue 2* (2005); 'Voyage' from *Images of Women* (Arrowhead Press, 2006).

Penelope Shuttle 'Missing you' from *Unsent: New and Selected Poems* (Bloodaxe, 2013).

Susan Jane Sims 'Bric à brac' from *Irene's Daughter* (Poetry Space Ltd., 2010).

Jonathan Steffen 'The colour of grief' from *The Colour of Love* (Acumen Publications, n.d.); 'In the chapel of rest' from *Acumen* (Acumen Publications, 2007).

Greta Stoddart 'The curtain' and 'Neuroblastoma' from *Poetry London* (n.d.).

Aeronwy Thomas 'Drowning' from *The Poetry Archive* (n.d.).

Tricia Torrington 'Desiderata' from *The Opium Fish* (Flarestock, 2010).

Katharine Towers 'The way we go' from *Poems on the underground* (n.d.).

Simon Tyler 'Where the Broken Sky Begins' from *A Packet of Poems* (Bradford on Avon Poetry Workshop and Ex Libris (n.d.).

Christine Vial 'Christmas Shopping with the Dead' from *Poetry Competition Anthology* (Norwich Writers, 2012); 'The Scattering' from *The Barnet Poetry Anthology* (Barnet Borough Arts Council, 2008).

Christine Webb 'Respite', 'Seven Weeks', 'Knowledge', 'Night Call', and 'Cannock Chase' from *Catching Your Breath* (Cinnamon Press, 2011).

Wynn Wheldon 'Last Words' from *Tiny Disturbances* (Acumen Publications, 2012).

Frances White 'Lullaby', 'The Black Cuillin' from *A Way With Words* (Poetry Monthly Press, 2007); 'Daffodils, I Suppose' from *20 Years of Merton Poets* (Merton Poets, 2010); 'The Gate' from *Lyrical beats* (Rhythm and Muse, 2012).

Merryn Williams 'This is Going to be One of Those Days' and 'The Trappings and the Suits of Woe' from *The First Wife's Tale* (Shoestring Press, 2007).

Emily Wills 'Red Primroses' from *Diverting The Sea* (The Rialto, 2000); 'Into Thin Air', 'Cove' and 'The Silence Afterwards' from *Developing the Negative* (The Rialto, 2008).

Margaret Wilmot 'Bone-meal, leaf-mould' from *Manchester Cathedral Anthology*, 2013

Stephen Wilson 'Amputation Clinic' and 'Your Last Story' from *Fluttering Hands* (Greenwich Exchange, 2008).

Anna Woodford 'Memento Mori' from *Birdhouse* (Salt Publishing, 2010).

Jeremy Young 'Snow' from *The Frogmore Papers No. 82 (2013);* 'Post Mortem' from *Quartos No. 50 (1995);* 'The Vocabulary of Hope' from *Riposte* (Edition 4, Volume 2 (1997).

Pam Zinnemann-Hope '*Todesengel*' from *On Cigarette Papers* (Ward Wood, 2014)